*Euro* *ne*

# GUILTLESS GOURMET

## GREEK, ENGLISH, GERMAN, RUSSIAN AND SCANDINAVIAN RECIPES FOR THE HEALTH-CONSCIOUS COOK

*Judy Gilliard & Joy Kirkpatrick R.D.*

European Cuisine from the Guiltless Gourmet: Greek, English, German, Russian, and Scandinavian Recipes for the Health-Conscious Cook © 1991
by Judy Gilliard and Joy Kirkpatrick, R.D.

**Library of Congress Cataloging-in-Publication Data**

Gilliard, Judy.
    European Cuisine from the Guiltless Gourmet:  Greek,
    English, German, Russian, and Scandinavian Recipes for
    the Health-Conscious Cook/Judy Gilliard and Joy
    Kirkpatrick, R.D.

Includes index

ISBN 0-937721-81-6      $11.95

Edited by:  Sandy McCullough, Donna Hoel
Illustrations:  Teri Gilliard
Photography:  William Bartlett, Thoen Photography
Stylist:  Darcy Reber
Production:  Nancy Nies
Printing:  Precision Graphics
Printed in the United States of America

10  9  8  7  6  5  4  3  2  1

Published by:
DCI/CHRONIMED Publishing
P.O. Box 47945
Minneapolis, MN 55447-9727

## DEDICATION

To our diabetic, weight conscious, and cholesterol-counting
friends whose encouragement and successes keep us going!

# ACKNOWLEDGMENTS

Our thanks to the following people:

For support and inspiration, Eleanor Kirkpatrick, Jeanne Jones, Nancy A. Washburn, Pete and Linda Spiers, Wendy Dunson, Sara Cookman, the Gilliards, the Hardacres, the Schweits, the Edgars, Izens, Cargills, George Kaskoutas, and Zorba's Restaurant.

To George Cleveland, David Wexler, Steve Crees, Donna Hoel, and the rest of the staff at DCI for believing in us.

To the Royal Cruise Line for allowing us to show their guests how to cruise and lose.

To the very special people at John F. Kennedy Memorial Hospital and KPSI Radio who allow us some time to write cookbooks.

To Naomi Guttman and Roberta Uhrich for a terrific program to work with.

To Ralph's Grocery Store, Jensen's, and Cafarelli's for always having our ingredients.

To Jan Mazza for her good eye.

A special thank you to Teri Gilliard for another round of great *Guiltless Gourmet* illustrations, and to Mona Virgillio and Neoma Ray for hours of inputting and computing.

## OUR TASTE TESTERS

Ron and Amanda Roisum, Patricia and Gregory Hook, Kathy and David Middleton, Jeff and Lisa Arakelian, Don Mead, George Lanning, Rod Murphy and his office staff, Sue Lawliss, Geri Whitney, Tom and Mona Virgillio, Frank and Michelle DiPietro, Kay Hazen, Becky Swanson, Kent Workley, Willy Vanderkolk, Sharon Carr, and Jan and Harvey Izen.

Nutrient analysis done with the Diet Wise program from Nutritional Data Resources, Willoughby, Ohio.

# Contents

# Hints About Ingredients

Here are some bits and pieces of information that may help to make your life easier as you become a Guiltless Gourmet. Understanding ingredients and measuring correctly are two important points in assuring successful results.

**Milk**—We almost always use nonfat milk, occasionally 1% if the recipe so states.

**Yogurt**—We use nonfat yogurt exclusively. Buy a good brand— try to find one without added gelatin.

**Yogurt cheese**—A delightful product you make from nonfat yogurt. When making yogurt cheese it is important to use a yogurt without added gelatin. See page 54 for recipe.

**Broths**—We use our recipe for Chicken Broth, page 53. You can also use the low-sodium granules or powder that call for adding hot water to reconstitute.

**Canned tomatoes**—Whenever possible buy the no-salt-added type. Read the labels carefully.

**Fructose**—We use granular fructose from the health food section in the grocery store. You can also purchase it in larger quantities from a health food store. It is important to keep fructose in a dry place as it easily absorbs moisture.

**Rice**—We use both brown rice and white rice. While we generally prefer brown rice, there are some occasions when white rice seems preferable.

**Sour cream**—We find that the newer reduced-calorie sour cream products work well. Be sure to use them in order to keep the total fat calories down.

**Cottage cheese**—We are very fond of the newer nonfat cottage cheeses that many dairies have available. Just another way to keep the fat calories down.

**Butter Buds**™—We have used Butter Buds™ for years and continue to find them a wonderful product. Each recipe using Butter Buds™ will indicate whether to use the dry form or the liquid form.

**Alcohol**—Various recipes use one kind of alcohol or another. In some cases it is certainly optional, in others it may be an important ingredient to enhance the flavor of the recipe.

**Cocoa powder**—We find that a good imported brand gives a smoother flavor to our recipes. If you cannot locate it in your regular market, a specialty store is bound to carry one or two brands.

# About Your Butcher

Life in the kitchen can become a lot easier when you find a good butcher. We like a small neighborhood butcher with an old-fashioned counter that has meats, poultry, and seafood. When you shop at a meat counter you can get just the amount you want, and the butcher can do much of your work for you.

Find out what days the seafood comes in and go in and buy it that day. Unless you are going to cook seafood that night, it is better to buy fresh frozen and keep it in the freezer until ready for use. It's always a good idea to order ahead if you're planning a dinner party. If there is anything special you want, given enough time ahead, the butcher can probably get it for you.

There is nothing like fresh, grade A, grain-fed chickens. In guiltless cooking we usually use boned, skinned chicken breasts. (You can have them wrap the bones in a separate package to use for broth or soups, if you wish.) We even have our butcher grind our chicken breast to save a little time.

You can choose the red meat you want and have it boned and well trimmed of fat. An example of how you can use the butcher to save you time and money: Buy a leg of lamb, have it boned and have part of it cut up for making kebabs. Have another part rolled and tied and use it instead of lamb loin.

Your butcher will probably have special package deals so you can buy in quantity. Be sure to tell him you only want lean, low-fat cuts. Your butcher will probably have ideas for you and your special needs, whether you are cooking for one or twenty-one. Always make sure you tell him if you are going to freeze any of your purchases so he can wrap it in freezer paper.

# Traveling in Guiltless Gourmet Style

Talking about European cuisine also makes us think of traveling to these delightful countries, so we thought we would give you some tips for watching those fat calories while traveling.

### Cruise to Lose . . . Weight, That Is!

Take a cruise? Who me? I'd be bored to tears, sitting around, playing bingo . . . not to mention the 10 pounds I'd gain! After all, what else is there to do on a cruise besides eat enormous amounts of outrageously fattening food?!

Sound familiar? That's where I thought cruising would take me until my travel agent convinced me to sail. Considering that I'm the type of person who is very uncomfortable in small places and can gain five pounds just looking at food, it took a certain amount of persuasion to get me on board. But alas, I surrendered and how this trip changed my opinion of travel forever!

As vice president and general manager of KPSI Radio in Palm Springs, California, my daily life is quite full. The combination of my career and my passion, writing *The Guiltless Gourmet* cookbooks, makes for a lifestyle of never-ending action. Cruising was a breakthrough! The total relaxation of the cruising environment and the many dynamic activities available have dispelled all my cruising fears.

And the weight gain? Not me...now, I Cruise to Lose!

Yes, everyone can control their weight while cruising and perhaps drop a few pounds in the process. Typically, the American diet includes skipping many meals and consuming a lot of high-fat foods. The best way to maintain your weight is to eat moderate portions of low-fat foods regularly—three to five times each day. Add exercise and you're on your way.

While many Americans are taking an interest in eating a more health conscious diet, having the proper foods available to them three to five times each day is difficult. The relaxed atmosphere of cruising allows you to concentrate on nutrition . . . and the food is readily accessible throughout the day! This makes cruising the perfect place to begin some healthy new eating habits.

Quite a few cruise lines are offering healthier food choices. Ask your travel agent or carefully examine the cruise line brochures. Look for menus that are approved by the American Heart Association. This is a clear indicator that the cruise line has taken an interest in healthy food offerings.

While items on an American Heart Association approved menu are guaranteed low in fat and cholesterol, you don't necessarily have to select these items to eat smart. Here, I'll share some tips with you that will send you ashore weighing less than when you boarded...and you won't miss one bit of on-board enjoyment.

1. *Alert the cruise line*. If you have certain dietary restrictions, notify the galley by writing in advance of your trip what specific requirements you would like to have met. Upon boarding, discuss these requirements with the head waiter.

Remember these waiters are trained in service, not nutrition. Tell the waiter just what you would like to eat and how you'd like it prepared. Once you discuss your needs with them, they'll be anxious to serve you and meet your demands happily. After all, throughout centuries, our culture has based a lot of happiness on food consumption.

2. *Plan your choices for the day*. Cruise lines publish the menu for each day the evening before. By reviewing this menu you can consider your choices in advance, which will eliminate a lot of temptation when you sit down to order your meal. If a Heart Association approved menu exists, ordering off that menu will make it easy to make the correct choice.

3. *Watch out for FATS*. The biggest culprits are foods laden with fat. Remember: Fat makes you fat. High- fat foods include butter and margarine, mayonnaise, cream, ice cream, cream soups and sauces, sweet rolls, cakes, pies, breakfast meats, red meat, and fried foods.

4. *Make choices*. You don't have to eliminate these completely. Limit your intake of high-fat foods to one portion each day (or even each meal), and you can enjoy a bit of forbidden food, yet maintain your weight.

For instance, if there is an excitingly rich dessert you absolutely must have, order a lighter item for your main course. If you are craving a juicy steak (or other red meat), have fresh fruit or sorbet for dessert. And if you plan ahead, knowing you're going to be eating a bit heavy, add a few extra minutes to your exercise routine.

5. **EXERCISE is crucial.** When you exercise you have increased energy and feel better. You will digest your meals better and you will look better.

On board there are many choices of exercise: walking or jogging the decks, swimming, taking exercise classes, and using the fitness equipment in the gym. So, swim an extra lap, or take the stairs everywhere you go on the ship to help you burn calories and fat and afford you an occasional exciting dessert or entree.

**Some Tried and True Guidelines:**

BREAKFAST: This list of choices will get you off to a good healthy start with lots of complex carbohydrates and little fat. Always have fresh fruit—skip the sweet rolls. Instead, stick to whole grain toast, or pancakes made with nonfat milk. Cereals, hot or cold, with nonfat milk are always a good choice. Only have eggs or Egg Beaters™ two times each week.

LUNCH OR DINNER: If choosing from the buffet, do a quick check of the entire buffet before you pick up your plate. Spend a moment thinking through a proper selection by balancing high-fat foods with more low-fat choices.

When seated at your table in the dining room, read through the entire menu before making any choices. Balance the heavier choices with the lighter foods. Always order your salad dressing and sauces on the side.

If there is something that you'd like and know would be a healthy, balanced choice, ask your waiter. Most of the time they are happy to help you choose your food by serving an appetizer, i.e. Shrimp Cocktail and Pasta with Tomato Sauce, as a main course.

DESSERT AND LIQUOR: When choosing dessert, stick to fresh fruit or sorbet as often as you can. Ask for a small dish of hot fudge to dip your fruit in. Of course, if there's a dessert you can't live without, plan ahead with lighter meal choices and . . . GO FOR IT!

Treat liquor as you would dessert. Enjoy it in moderation. If you're having a cocktail before dinner, be sure to modify your food plan for that meal. Beware of culprit snacks high in salt and fat that may be sitting on the bar. One drink can lower your will power and the temptation to pop a handful of nuts in your mouth can take over. If sweet after-dinner drinks are your desire, have one in place of dessert.

Consider trying nonalcoholic drinks. Today all sorts of people are eliminating liquor from their diets by drinking mineral water with lemon or lime. If you crave a certain drink, contemplate a Virgin Mary, Virgin Daiquiri or other such "virgin" drinks. You'll never miss the alcohol. NEVER order cream drinks. Cream equals FAT! And, remember that alcohol calories are empty calories!

Good alcohol choices include Brut champagne, dry wines and spritzers, and dry vermouth on the rocks.

SNACKS AND THE MIDNIGHT BUFFET: Use the same guide-lines above, watch your choices and your portions, and ENJOY!

By following this plan, you'll Cruise to Lose, you'll get proper nutrition, and have more energy to enjoy all the wonderful things cruising has to offer.

# Greek Cuisine

# GREECE

The Greek people are among the friendliest in the world.  They are warm and outgoing, with a great love of life—that flows over into a great love of food.  On a recent two week cruise on the Royal Cruise Line, we spent over a week in the Greek Isles.  The crew of the ship was Greek, so naturally we've chosen to share some of our favorite Greek foods.

The secret to Greek cooking is the subtle flavors, often from fresh herbs and spices.  It's fairly easy to modify fat content without sacrificing flavor.  You'll be surprised to see how low in fat and calories the Greek dishes are.  So read on and set up your kitchen for great Greek cooking.

## Setting Up Your Greek Kitchen

### *Herbs and spices*

Fresh is always best.  When you can't find fresh, buy whole dried herbs and crush them with a mortar and pestle just before using.  The rule of thumb is one part fresh is equal to 3 parts dried.

Allspice (Buy ground, since it's very hard to grind yourself.)
Cinnamon (Buy ground.)
Cloves (Buy ground.)
Dillweed
Garlic, fresh cloves and powdered
Mint
Oregano
Thyme
Parsley (Buy fresh and chop in food processor.  Keep in the freezer.)
Basil
Bay leaves
Cumin (Buy whole seeds and keep in a grinder.)
Lemon peel, fresh grated (Keep in freezer.)
Black pepper
Cayenne

***Basic ingredients used in Greek cooking.***
(This is a good basic list of items to have on hand to whip up a
Greek dish at a moment's notice.)

Feta cheese
Nonfat plain yogurt
Orzo pasta
Phyllo dough (Found in the freezer in most supermarkets.)
Brown and white rice
Lemons
Low-salt chicken broth (page 53)
Onions
Bell peppers (all colors)
Eggplant
Honey
Walnuts
Wine vinegars
Butter Buds™
Cream of Rice cereal™
Fructose
All-purpose flour
Cucumbers
Tomatoes, diced and whole
Lettuce
Fresh fruits

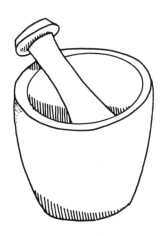

# Greek Easter Brunch

Greek Easter is one of the most celebrated of all holidays. After going to church, the Greeks break a long fast with lots of wonderful food. What fun to change the pace from a more traditionally American Easter brunch or dinner to a Greek-style festival of foods.

Start with your decor. Greek colors are blue and white—an easy and fun combination to work with. Use your white dishes and serving pieces with blue table cloths and napkins. Your center piece can be a fresh fruit basket. Place a loaf of Greek Easter bread on a cutting board on the table. Most bakeries will have Greek Easter bread, but you may need to order it ahead. Also order fresh-baked pita bread.

Greek music is a must and really creates the warm, fun-loving atmosphere. You can't miss with the soundtrack from *Zorba the Greek*, but your favorite record store probably has lots of suggestions. For a really festive event, contact a local Greek restaurant or Greek church for the names of musicians who might come to play for you.

The beverages for your Easter brunch could include the Greek wine, Resina, mixed with soda water and a twist of lemon. Mineral water with a twist of lemon is always appropriate. With dessert, serve a strong coffee and offer Mataxa (Greek brandy) or ouzo (licorice-flavored liquor).

# Menu

### Appetizers

Eggplant Caviar
Humus
(Serve both with pita bread)

Chicken Lemon Soup
(Serve in coffee mugs as your guests are milling about)

### Buffet

Pear and Lettuce Salad
Greek Salad

Stuffed Zucchini
Oven-Fried Eggplant with Cucumber Yogurt Salad

Pastitsio
Turkey Breast Marinated with Lemon and Herbs
Lamb Loin

Greek Easter Bread

### Dessert

Honey Yogurt Cake
Fresh Fruit

Coffee

# Eggplant Caviar

This is an excellent dish to have on hand. It's very low in calories and can be served as a dip with crackers at cocktail time, stuffed in pita bread for lunch, or served on lettuce leaves and garnished with chopped tomatoes and cucumbers as a first course at dinner.

    2  *medium eggplants*
    1  *teaspoon olive oil*
    1  *medium onion, diced*
    2  *cloves garlic, minced*
    1  *red bell pepper, diced*
    1  *tablespoon fresh chopped parsley*
  1/2  *teaspoon ground black pepper*
    1  *tablespoon fresh lemon juice*
    3  *teaspoons capers*

1. Preheat oven to 400 degrees.
2. Bake whole eggplants for 1 hour. Let cool until you can handle them.
3. Heat olive oil in a skillet and saute onion, garlic, and red bell pepper until soft.
4. Cut eggplants in half, scoop out the pulp, and put pulp in food processor with steel blade. Add onion mixture and pulsate 4 times. Add parsley, black pepper, lemon juice, and capers and pulsate 2 to 4 times, until mixture is well mixed.
5. Place in a covered container and refrigerate at least 6 hours before serving. (Best if refrigerated overnight.)

Makes 8 servings.

*Each serving contains:*
     21  *calories*
      0  *grams protein*
      4  *grams carbohydrate*        *ADA Exchange Value:*
         *negligible grams fat*          1  *Vegetable*
    308  *mgs. sodium*                    *Negligible fat*
      0  *mgs. cholesterol*               *calories.*
      1  *gram dietary fiber*

EUROPEAN CUISINE FROM THE GUILTLESS GOURMET

# Humus

This is an excellent source of protein and can be very versatile as a dip with crackers and vegetables or as a sandwich spread.

   1   *cup dried chickpeas*
   3   *tablespoons fresh lemon juice*
   2   *cloves garlic, peeled*
   $1/2$   *cup tahini butter*
   $1/2$   *teaspoon cayenne pepper*
        *Fresh chopped parsley to garnish*

1. Soak chickpeas overnight, then rinse.
2. In a large saucepan, cover chickpeas with water and bring to boil.  Cover and simmer 1 hour or until tender.
3. Drain cooked chickpeas, reserving 1 cup of the liquid.
4. In a food processor with a steel blade, process garlic cloves until they are stuck to the sides.
5. Add remaining ingredients, except parsley, to food processor, and process until smooth.
6. Put mixture in a covered bowl and refrigerate at least 6 hours before serving.  Garnish with chopped parsley.

Makes 10 servings.  1 serving = $1/2$ cup

*Each serving contains:*
   107   *calories*
     5   *grams protein*
     8   *grams carbohydrate*
     7   *grams fat*
    75   *mgs. sodium*
     0   *mgs. cholesterol*
     2   *grams dietary fiber*

*ADA Exchange Value:*
   $1/2$   *Starch/Bread*
   1 $1/2$   *Fat*
   59%   *of total calories are from fat.*

# Yogurt Soup

This is a perfect start to a summer evening meal.  The flavors mingle so well together, you would never guess the walnuts are there.  But you don't want to make it without them!

    2   *cloves garlic, peeled*
  1/2   *cup walnuts*
    1   *tablespoon white wine vinegar*
    3   *cups plain nonfat yogurt*
    1   *cup 1 percent milk*
  1/2   *teaspoon white pepper*
    1   *cucumber, peeled, seeded, and diced*
        *Fresh chopped parsley to garnish*

1. In a food processor with steel blades, drop garlic in and run until all garlic has stuck to sides.
2. Add walnuts and vinegar, process until nuts are finely chopped.
3. Add yogurt, milk, and white pepper.  Blend until smooth.
4. Pour into bowl, add cucumbers, and refrigerate at least 4 hours before serving.
5. Garnish with chopped parsley.

Makes 8 servings.

**Each serving contains:**

    103   calories
      7   grams protein
     10   grams carbohydrate
      4   grams fat
     75   mgs. sodium
      6   mgs. cholesterol
      0   grams dietary fiber

**ADA Exchange Value:**

  1/2   **Milk**
  1/2   **Vegetable**
    1   **Fat**
  35%   **of total calories are from fat.**

# Spinach and Lentil Soup

 1   *cup large brown lentils*
7 ¹/₂  *cups low-salt Chicken Broth (page 53)*
 1   *teaspoon olive oil*
 1   *large onion, chopped*
 2   *10-ounce boxes frozen spinach, thawed, with*
     *water squeezed out*
 2   *tablespoons tomato paste*
¹/₄  *teaspoon cayenne pepper*
 1   *tablespoon chopped fresh oregano*

1. Put lentils and chicken broth in a large saucepan. Bring to boil, reduce heat, and simmer, uncovered, 1 hour or until lentils are tender.
2. Heat oil in a skillet. Add onions and saute until golden. Add spinach and tomato paste. Mix together over low heat until warm.
3. Add mixture to lentils. Add cayenne pepper, and oregano. Cover and simmer 20 minutes. If soup becomes too thick, add more water.

Makes 6 servings.

**Each serving contains:**
114  *calories*
  7  *grams protein*
 15  *grams carbohydrate*
  4  *grams fat*
300  *mgs. sodium*
  1  *mg. cholesterol*
  4  *grams dietary fiber*

**ADA Exchange Value:**
 1  *Starch/Bread*
 1  *Fat*
32%  *of total calories are from fat.*

# Chicken Lemon Soup (Augoremone)

  6   cups low-salt Chicken Broth (page 53)
²/₃   cup white rice
  1   egg
  2   egg whites
      Juice of 2 lemons

1. Bring broth to boil, add rice, cover, and simmer 20 minutes.
2. Beat egg and egg whites together. Add a little of the hot broth and beat. Slowly add eggs to hot broth and stir until thickened.
3. Stir in lemon juice and serve.

Makes 6 servings.

*Each serving contains:*

     60   calories
      3   grams protein
      9   grams carbohydrate
      1   gram fat
    280   mgs. sodium
     26   mgs. cholesterol
      0   grams dietary fiber

*ADA Exchange Value:*

    ¹/₂   Starch/Bread
    ¹/₂   Lean Meat
    15%   of total calories are from fat.

# Greek Tomato Sauce

Tomatoes are the secret ingredient in this special sauce. Use imported canned Italian plum tomatoes. They are easily found in most supermarkets.

> 2 *teaspoons olive oil*
> 3 *cloves minced garlic*
> 2 *onions, chopped*
> 2 *32-ounce cans whole Italian plum tomatoes*
> 1 *6-ounce can tomato paste*
> 2 *tablespoons chopped fresh oregano*
>   *(2 teaspoons dried)*
> $^1/_2$ *teaspoon ground black pepper*
> $^1/_2$ *teaspoon fructose*

1. Heat olive oil in a large Dutch oven. Add garlic and onions and saute until soft.
2. Add the remaining ingredients. With a potato masher, mash the tomatoes slightly. Bring to a boil, stirring constantly. Reduce heat and simmer, uncovered, 1 hour, stirring frequently.

Makes 7 cups of sauce, or about 8 servings.

*Each serving contains:*
> 74 *calories*
> 3 *grams protein*
> 14 *grams carbohydrate*
> 2 *grams fat*
> 38 *mgs. sodium*
> 0 *mgs. cholesterol*
> 2 *grams dietary fiber*

*ADA Exchange Value:*
> 3 *Vegetable*
> 24% *of total calories are from fat.*

# Greek Salad

1   *head Boston lettuce*
1   *medium English cucumber, sliced*
2   *medium tomatoes, cut in wedges*
2   *medium green bell peppers, cut in slices*
1   *tablespoon minced fresh oregano*
3   *tablespoons red wine vinegar*
$^1/_2$   *teaspoon black pepper*
4   *ounces crumbled feta cheese*

1. Wash and dry lettuce, keeping leaves whole.  Line a platter or shallow bowl with leaves.
2. Mix cucumber, tomato wedges, and bell pepper slices together.
3. Mix oregano, vinegar, and pepper together and toss gently with vegetable mixture.
4. Place vegetables on top of the lettuce leaves and sprinkle with feta cheese.

Makes 6 servings.

*Each serving contains:*
     77   *calories*
      4   *grams protein*
      7   *grams carbohydrate*
      4   *grams fat*
   217   *mgs. sodium*
    16   *mgs. cholesterol*
      4   *grams dietary fiber*

*ADA Exchange Value:*
     1   *Vegetable*
     1   *Fat*
  48%   *of total calories are from fat.*

# Pear and Lettuce Salad

This is so simple, yet its light, refreshing taste adds the perfect touch to a meal.

> 1 head Romaine lettuce
> 2 pears
> 1 tablespoon lemon juice in 1 cup water
> $^1/_4$ cup pear nectar
> 3 tablespoons pear vinegar or white wine vinegar

1. Wash Romaine well, cut in bite-sized pieces, and spin dry in a salad spinner.
2. Cut pears in chunks and toss in lemon juice to keep them from turning brown.
3. Mix pear nectar and vinegar together.
4. Toss lettuce, pears, and dressing together.

Makes 6 servings.

*Each serving contains:*

> 58 calories
> 1 gram protein
> 14 grams carbohydrate
> 0 grams fat
> 4 mgs. sodium
> 0 mgs. cholesterol
> 2 grams dietary fiber

*ADA Exchange Value:*

> $^1/_2$ Fruit
> 1 Vegetable
> Negligible fat calories.

# Tomato Cucumber Salad

  3  *large tomatoes, cut in wedges*
  1  *medium English cucumber, sliced*
  3  *scallions, chopped fine, including tops*
     *Juice of 1 lemon*
  2  *teaspoons fresh oregano ($^1/_2$ teaspoon dried)*
 $^1/_4$  *teaspoon ground black pepper*
  1  *tablespoon olive oil*

1. Put tomatoes, cucumbers, and scallions in a bowl.
2. Mix lemon juice, oregano, pepper, and olive oil together.
3. Toss dressing into vegetables just before serving.

Makes 6 servings.

*Each serving contains:*
- 42  *calories*
-  0  *grams protein*
-  5  *grams carbohydrate*
-  3  *grams fat*
-  8  *mgs. sodium*
-  0  *mgs. cholesterol*
-  2  *grams dietary fiber*

*ADA Exchange Value:*
-  1  *Vegetable*
- $^1/_2$  *Fat*
- 64%  *of total calories are from fat.*

# Cucumber Yogurt Salad

This can be served as a condiment or on a bed of lettuce as a salad.

> 2 cups Yogurt Cheese (page 54)
> 1 large cucumber, peeled, seeded, and coarsely grated
> 3 cloves garlic, crushed
> 1 teaspoon dried dill weed (1 tablespoon fresh dill)
> $1/2$ teaspoon ground white pepper
> Thickly sliced cucumber and fresh dill for garnish

1. Mix first 5 ingredients together and chill for 2 hours.
2. Garnish with cucumber and fresh dill.

Makes 8 servings.

*Each serving contains:*
> 72 calories
> 6 grams protein
> 10 grams carbohydrate
> 1 gram fat
> 81 mgs. sodium
> 3 mgs. cholesterol
> 1 gram dietary fiber

*ADA Exchange Value:*
> $1/2$ Milk
> 1 Vegetable
> 13% of total calories are from fat.

# Orzo Pilaf

Orzo is a rice-shaped pasta that is often used in Greek cooking.

3 *cups water seasoned with 2 tablespoons low-salt chicken granules*
1 *cup orzo*
1 *clove garlic, minced*
1 *small onion, chopped*
2 *medium carrots, grated*
1/2 *medium green bell pepper, chopped*

1. Bring water to boil.  Add orzo.  Cook for 10 minutes.  Drain.
2. In a saute pan sprayed with a nonstick cooking spray, saute garlic and all the vegetables together until soft.
3. Mix orzo into vegetables and transfer to a serving dish.  This can be set aside and reheated in the microwave just before serving.

Makes 6 servings.

*Each serving contains:*
55 *calories*
2 *grams protein*
11 *grams carbohydrate*
0 *grams fat*
20 *mgs. sodium*
1 *mg. cholesterol*
1 *gram dietary fiber*

*ADA Exchange Value:*
1/2 *Starch/Bread*
1 *Vegetable*
*negligible fat calories.*

# Stuffed Eggplant

3   small eggplants
1   medium onion, chopped
1   clove garlic, minced
$1/2$   pound lean ground lamb or beef
2   cups cooked brown rice
1   tablespoon chopped fresh oregano (2 teaspoons dried)
$1/4$   teaspoon ground allspice
$1/2$   teaspoon ground black pepper
1   14-ounce can diced tomatoes, drained
    Chopped fresh parsley

1. Preheat oven to 350 degrees. Wrap eggplants in foil and bake 20 minutes. Cool.
2. Cut eggplants in half and scoop out pulp, leaving $1/2$-inch border to make a shell.
3. In a large skillet sprayed with a nonstick spray, saute onion and garlic until soft. Add the eggplant pulp and cook for 10 minutes. Remove from skillet and set aside.
4. Brown the meat in the skillet. Drain meat in colander lined with paper towel to remove excess fat.
5. Add all ingredients to skillet and mix well.
6. Fill eggplant shells with mixture. Place in a baking pan and bake for 20 minutes.

Makes 6 servings.

**Each serving contains:**
  178   calories
   12   grams protein
   27   grams carbohydrate
    3   grams fat
   31   mgs. sodium
   24   mgs. cholesterol
    3   grams dietary fiber

**ADA Exchange Value:**
    1   Lean Meat,  1 Starch/Bread
    2   Vegetable
  15%   of total calories are from fat.

# Oven-Fried Eggplant

Here's a crispy, tender way to cook eggplant.

> 1 *medium-to-large eggplant cut in ¹/₄-inch rounds*
> ¹/₂ *cup unbleached flour*
> 2 *egg whites slightly beaten with ¹/₄ cup water*
> 2 *cups plain bread crumbs*
> ¹/₂ *teaspoon dry oregano*
> ¹/₂ *teaspoon garlic powder*
> ¹/₄ *teaspoon ground black pepper*

1. Preheat oven to 350 degrees.
2. In a large pot of boiling water, blanch eggplant for 3 minutes in small batches.
3. Combine bread crumbs, oregano, garlic powder, and pepper.
4. Dip eggplant first in flour, then in egg whites, ending with bread crumb mixture.
5. Place dipped eggplant on a cookie sheet sprayed with a nonstick cooking spray. Bake for 15 minutes.

Makes 6 servings.

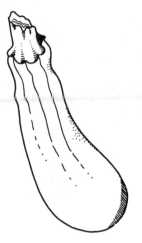

*Each serving contains:*
> 178 *calories*
> 7 *grams protein*
> 33 *grams carbohydrate*
> 2 *grams fat*
> 262 *mgs. sodium*
> 2 *mgs. cholesterol*
> 1 *gram dietary fiber*

*ADA Exchange Value:*
> 2 *Starch/Bread*
> 10% *of total calories are from fat.*

# Stuffed Zucchini

6   *medium zucchini*
1   *medium onion, chopped*
1   *teaspoon ground cumin*
1   *tablespoon chopped fresh parsley*
*¹/₂*   *cup cooked brown rice*
*¹/₂*   *teaspoon ground black pepper*

1. Preheat oven to 350 degrees.
2. Cut ends off zucchini. Blanch in boiling water 3 minutes.
3. With a grapefruit spoon or a melon baller, scoop the middle out of the zucchini, forming a tunnel, and set aside.
4. In a skillet sprayed with a nonstick spray, saute the onion until soft. Add the zucchini that you scooped out, cumin, parsley, brown rice, and pepper and mix together.
5. Fill the zucchini boats with the mixture. Bake for 10 minutes.

Makes 6 servings.

*Each serving contains:*
    51   *calories*
     2   *grams protein*
    11   *grams carbohydrate*
     0   *grams fat*
     4   *mgs. sodium*
     0   *mgs. cholesterol*
     2   *grams dietary fiber*

*ADA Exchange Value:*
     2   *Vegetable*
         *negligible fat calories.*

# Shrimp with Tomato and Feta Cheese

1 ¹/₂  *pounds shrimp (16 to a pound)*
   1  *tablespoon olive oil*
   1  *medium onion, chopped*
  ¹/₂  *cup dry white wine (or vermouth)*
   1  *27-ounce can diced tomatoes with juice*
   2  *tablespoons fresh chopped parsley*
  ¹/₂  *teaspoon oregano*
  ¹/₄  *teaspoon ground pepper*
  ¹/₄  *pound crumbled feta cheese*

1. Clean and rinse shrimp, pat dry, and set aside.
2. Heat oil in large skillet and saute onion until soft.
3. Stir in wine, tomatoes, parsley, oregano, and pepper.  Bring to boil and cook until mixture thickens slightly.
4. Add shrimp and cook over medium heat until shrimp are done (10 to 15 minutes).
5. Stir in feta cheese.

Makes 6 servings.

*Each serving contains:*
   134  *calories*
     7  *grams protein*
     9  *grams carbohydrate*
     7  *grams fat*
   252  *mgs. sodium*
    37  *mgs. cholesterol*
     1  *gram dietary fiber*

*ADA Exchange Value:*
   1  *Lean Meat*
   2  *Vegetable*
   1  *Fat*
  47%  *of total calories are from fat.*

# Halibut on Skewers

This dish has a very delicate flavor, and even people who don't normally eat fish like it!  Be sure to serve it with the bay leaves—you don't eat them, but they make a more interesting presentation.  If there is any fish left over, it's great served cold in a salad.

- *¹/₂ medium onion, chopped fine*
- *1 tablespoon fresh lemon juice, plus 2 tablespoons water*
- *¹/₂ teaspoon ground white pepper*
- *1 ¹/₂ pounds halibut cut into 1-inch cubes*
- *24 large bay leaves*

1. Mix onion, lemon juice, and pepper in a bowl.
2. Gently add the fish, coating all sides.  Cover tightly and refrigerate 4 hours.
3. Put bay leaves in a pot of boiling water.  Turn off heat and let stand 1 hour.  Drain.
4. Thread fish cubes and bay leaves alternately on skewers.
5. Barbeque on grill or cook under broiler 10 to 15 minutes.

Makes 6 servings.

*Each serving contains:*
- *169 calories*
- *30 grams protein*
- *2 grams carbohydrate*
- *3 grams fat*
- *82 mgs. sodium*
- *48 mgs. cholesterol*
- *0 grams dietary fiber*

*ADA Exchange Value:*
- *4 Lean Meat*
- *17% of total calories are from fat.*

# Lemon Chicken

6 chicken breast halves, skinned and left on bone
1 small onion cut in thin strips
2 sticks celery cut in julienne strips
2 carrots, cut in julienne strips
1 tablespoon fresh chopped basil ($^{1}/_{2}$ teaspoon dried)
1 bay leaf
  Juice and rind of 2 small lemons
$^{1}/_{2}$ cup water
$^{1}/_{2}$ teaspoon ground black pepper

1. In a large saute pan sprayed with a nonstick cooking spray, brown chicken breasts, meat side down. Remove and set aside.
2. Add onions, celery, and carrots. Cook over medium heat until soft.
3. Add basil, bay leaf, lemon juice and rind, water, and pepper. Mix and bring to a boil.
4. Reduce heat to simmer. Add chicken, bone side down. Cover and cook until done, about 30 to 45 minutes.
5. Remove chicken and vegetables to a serving platter. Bring remaining sauce to a boil to thicken. Pour over chicken.

Makes 6 servings.

*Each serving contains:*

160 *calories*
 25 *grams protein*
  6 *grams carbohydrate*
  3 *grams fat*
221 *mgs. sodium*
 69 *mgs. cholesterol*
  1 *gram dietary fiber*

   *ADA Exchange Value*
  2 *Lean Meat*
  1 *Vegetable*
17% *of total calories are from fat.*

# Moussaka

This is a traditional Greek dish usually prepared with ground lamb or beef and covered with a thick white sauce. Here we replaced the white sauce with our own low-fat version and used ground chicken to reduce the fat content even more. You can use beef or lamb in this recipe or a combination of red meat and chicken, but remember you will be increasing your fat calories.

 2  *large eggplants cut into ¼-inch round slices*
 1  *teaspoon olive oil*
 2  *medium onions, chopped*
 1 ½ *pounds chicken breast meat, ground*
 1  *27-ounce can diced tomatoes in juice*
 ½  *cup chopped fresh parsley*
 ¼  *teaspoon ground cinnamon*
 ½  *teaspoon ground nutmeg*
 1  *tablespoon fresh oregano (½ teaspoon dry oregano)*
 1  *cup plain nonfat yogurt*

*Greek White Sauce*
 3  *cups nonfat milk*
 2  *teaspoons dry Butter Buds™*
 ½  *teaspoon ground white pepper*
 ¾  *cup Cream of Rice™ cereal*
 ¼  *cup Parmesan cheese*

1. Preheat oven to 400 degrees.
2. Lay eggplant slices on paper towels for 45 minutes, turning once. Place eggplant on cookie sheet and bake for 15 minutes. Remove eggplant from oven and reduce oven heat to 350.
3. Heat olive oil in a nonstick skillet. Add onion and saute until soft. Remove onions from pan and set aside.
4. Saute chicken in same skillet until almost cooked. Add onions, tomatoes with juice, parsley, cinnamon, nutmeg, and oregano. Mix and simmer uncovered for 30 minutes.
5. Stir in yogurt.

6. Spray a baking pan with a nonstick spray. Layer eggplant on the bottom. Top with chicken mixture.
7. Put milk, Butter Buds™, and white pepper in a saucepan. Bring to boil. Slowly add Cream of Rice™, stirring constantly. Add Parmesan cheese. When sauce is thick, pour over the moussaka.
8. Bake at 350 degrees for 45 minutes. Let stand 10 minutes before serving.

Makes 8 servings.

*Each serving contains:*

|     |                       |
| --- | --------------------- |
| 264 | *calories*            |
| 34  | *grams protein*       |
| 20  | *grams carbohydrate*  |
| 5   | *grams fat*           |
| 323 | *mgs. sodium*         |
| 7   | *mgs. cholesterol*    |
| 3   | *grams dietary fiber* |

*ADA Exchange Value:*

|       |                                  |
| ----- | -------------------------------- |
| 3     | *Lean Meat*                      |
| 1/2   | *Starch/Bread*                   |
| 1/2   | *Milk*                           |
| 2     | *Vegetable*                      |
| 17%   | *of total calories are from fat.* |

# Pastitsio

1   pound lean ground beef
1   small onion, chopped
1   27-ounce can diced tomatoes, with juice
3   tablespoons chopped fresh parsley
$^1/_2$   teaspoon cinnamon
$^1/_2$   teaspoon ground black pepper
1   pound ziti
4   egg whites
$^1/_2$   cup Parmesan cheese
    Greek White Sauce (page 41)

1. Preheat oven to 350 degrees.
2. In a nonstick skillet, brown beef. Remove from pan and set
   aside on paper towel to drain excess fat. In skillet, saute
   onion until soft. Return meat to pan and mix with onion.
3. Add tomatoes with juice, parsley, cinnamon, and pepper. Mix
   and simmer 15 minutes, uncovered.
4. Cook ziti in boiling water until slightly underdone. Drain well.
5. Slightly whip egg whites and mix into ziti, along with 1/4 cup
   Parmesan cheese.
6. In a baking pan sprayed with a nonstick spray, spread ziti
   mixture and press down with a wooden spoon or your hand.
7. Top with meat mixture, then with Greek White Sauce.
   Sprinkle with remaining cheese.
8. Bake for 45 minutes. Let stand 10 to 15 minutes before
   serving.

Makes 8 servings.

*Each serving contains:*
- 365   calories
- 25   grams protein
- 39   grams carbohydrate
- 12   grams fat
- 166   mgs. sodium
- 52   mgs. cholesterol
- 2   grams dietary fiber

*ADA Exchange Value:*
- 2   Lean Meat
- 1   Medium-Fat Meat
- 2   Starch/Bread
- 2   Vegetable
- 30%   of total calories are from fat.

EUROPEAN CUISINE FROM THE GUILTLESS GOURMET

# Spinach Cheese Pie (Spanakopita)

    6  sheets frozen filo dough, thawed
  $1/2$  cup low-salt Chicken Broth (page 53)
   10  ounces frozen chopped spinach, thawed, with
       water squeezed out
    3  ounces crumbled feta cheese
$1 1/2$  cups low-fat ricotta cheese
    2  egg whites, slightly beaten
    1  tablespoon minced fresh oregano (1 teaspoon
       dried)
  $1/2$  teaspoon ground black pepper
       Pinch of nutmeg

1. Spray a 9-inch pie pan or spring-form pan with a nonstick spray.
2. Put the chicken broth in a spray bottle.
3. Mix spinach, feta cheese, ricotta cheese, egg whites, oregano, pepper, and nutmeg.
4. In the bottom of your pie plate place 4 sheets of the filo dough one at a time, spraying each with the Chicken Broth. Line up the dough with the sides of the pan and fold over any excess dough into the bottom of the pan. You have to work quickly because the filo dries out fast.
5. Spoon the spinach mixture into the pan. Cover with the remaining 2 sheets of filo, again spraying each with the chicken broth.
6. Bake in a preheated oven, 400 degrees for 40 minutes.

Makes 6 servings.

Each serving contains:

| | | ADA Exchange Value: | |
|---|---|---|---|
| 170 | calories | | |
| 13 | grams protein | 2 | Lean Meat |
| 12 | grams carbohydrate | $1/2$ | Starch/Bread |
| 8 | grams fat | 1 | Vegetable |
| 414 | mgs. sodium | 42% | of total |
| 132 | mgs. cholesterol | | calories are |
| 2 | grams dietary fiber | | from fat. |

# Stuffed Peppers

  6  *medium red or green bell peppers*
  1  *medium onion, chopped*
 12  *ounces lean ground beef or lamb*
  1  *tablespoon chopped fresh dill (1 teaspoon dried)*
  2  *tablespoons fresh lemon juice*
  1  *teaspoon ground black pepper*
  1  *cup cooked brown rice*
  3  *cups Greek Tomato Sauce (page 29)*

1. Preheat oven to 350 degrees.
2. Wash peppers and blanch in boiling water 3 minutes. Remove and cool.
3. Cut 1 inch off the tops of each pepper. Remove core and seeds. Trim bottoms so peppers will stand up.
4. In a skillet sprayed with a nonstick spray, cook onion until soft. Remove from pan and set aside.
5. In the skillet, brown the meat well and drain in a colander lined with paper towel to remove excess fat.
6. Add onions, meat, and the remaining ingredients (except for tomato sauce) to skillet. Mix well.
7. Fill peppers with meat mixture and put tops on. Place in a baking dish half filled with water. Cover loosely with foil. Bake 45 minutes.
8. Remove with slotted spoon to a serving platter. Top each pepper with 1/2 cup tomato sauce that has been heated.

Makes 6 servings.

**Each serving contains:**

| | |
|---|---|
| 231 *calories* | **ADA Exchange Value:** |
| 17 *grams protein* | 2 *Lean Meat* |
| 27 *grams carbohydrate* | 1 *Starch/Bread* |
| 7 *grams fat* | 2 *Vegetable* |
| 64 *mgs. sodium* | 27% *of total* |
| 36 *mgs. cholesterol* | *calories are* |
| 4 *grams dietary fiber* | *from fat.* |

# Turkey Breast Marinated with Lemon and Herbs

This is also excellent cooked on the grill.

> 2 *pounds boneless, skinless turkey breast*
> *Juice and grated rind of 2 lemons*
> 1 *teaspoon oregano*
> *Pinch cumin*
> 1 *tablespoon chopped fresh parsley*
> 1/2 *teaspoon thyme*
> 1/2 *teaspoon ground white pepper*

1. Preheat oven to 325 degrees.
2. Rinse and pat turkey breast dry.
3. Mix remaining ingredients.
4. Coat all sides of turkey breast with marinade.  Cover and refrigerate overnight, if possible, or no less than 4 hours.
5. Roast, covered, for 35 minutes per pound (one hou,r 10 minutes for two-pound breast).  Roast uncovered for last 10 minutes or until the temperature inside the turkey reaches 170 degrees.

Makes 8 servings.

*Each serving contains:*
> 158 *calories*
> 31 *grams protein*
> *negligible grams carbohydrate*
> 4 *grams fat*
> 73 *mgs. sodium*
> 8 *mgs. cholesterol*
> *negligible grams dietary fiber*

*ADA Exchange Value:*
> 4 *Lean Meat*
> 23% *of total calories are from fat.*

# Shish Kebab

*Marinade*

- 1 *medium clove garlic, minced*
- 1 *tablespoon minced fresh oregano (1 teaspoon dried)*
- 1 *teaspoon minced fresh rosemary ($1/4$ teaspoon dried)*
- $1/3$ *cup dry white wine or dry vermouth*
- $1/2$ *teaspoon fresh ground pepper*
- 2 *tablespoons red wine vinegar*

1. Mix all ingredients.

- 1 $1/2$ *pounds very lean lamb cut in 1-inch cubes*
- 2 *medium onions cut in half, with wedges separated in layers of 2 each*
- 3 *bell peppers (green, yellow, and red) cut in fourths*
- 16 *mushrooms, washed*

1. Soak the lamb cubes in marinade for 2 to 6 hours.
2. On a skewer, alternate lamb, onion, pepper, and mushrooms.
3. Grill or cook under broiler to desired doneness.

Makes 6 servings.

*Each serving contains:*

- 237 *calories*
- 28 *grams protein*
- 7 *grams carbohydrate*
- 10 *grams fat*
- 69 *mgs. sodium*
- 52 *mgs. cholesterol*
- 2 *grams dietary fiber*

*ADA Exchange Value:*

- 4 *Lean Meat*
- 1 *Vegetable*
- 38% *of total calories are from fat.*

# Lamb Loin

Whenever you can, grill your meat. It's a healthy way to cook and your guests will love it. This lamb dish is perfect for the outdoor grill.

1 ¹/₂ **pounds loin of lamb, boned, trimmed, and tied**
2 **tablespoons fresh lemon juice**
2 **cloves garlic, crushed**
1 ¹/₂ **teaspoons fresh oregano ( ¹/₂ teaspoon dry)**
1 ¹/₂ **teaspoons fresh thyme ( ¹/₂ teaspoon dry)**
¹/₄ **teaspoon pepper**

1. Mix all ingredients (except lamb) together and rub on lamb. Wrap tightly and refrigerate 4 to 6 hours.
2. Grill or roast in a 350-degree oven to desired doneness. (Medium rare is about 11 minutes on each side.)

Makes 6 servings.

*Each serving contains:*
217 *calories*
33 *grams protein*
1 *gram carbohydrate*
8 *grams fat*
82 *mgs. sodium*
68 *mgs. cholesterol*
0 *grams dietary fiber*

*ADA Exchange Value:*
4 *Lean Meat*
33% *of total calories are from fat.*

# Honey Cakes

   3  cups all-purpose flour, sifted
   1  teaspoon baking powder
   1  teaspoon baking soda
   1  cup nonfat plain yogurt
 1/4  cup fructose
 1/2  cup cognac
   4  tablespoons orange juice
   1  tablespoon orange rind
 1/2  cup honey
 1/2  cup finely chopped walnuts
   1  teaspoon ground cinnamon

1. Sift flour, baking powder, and baking soda together.
2. Combine yogurt, fructose, cognac, orange juice, and rind.
3. Slowly add flour to the yogurt mixture and mix until all ingredients are combined.
4. Spray a cookie sheet with nonstick spray. Shape dough into 24 balls. Place balls well apart on the cookie sheet and press down with a spoon. Bake 20 minutes at 350 degrees. Cool on baking sheet.
5. In a small bowl, heat honey slightly in microwave. (This makes it less sticky.) Mix walnuts and cinnamon together and put on a plate. Dip the capes into the honey, then the walnuts.

Makes 12 servings.

*Each serving contains:*
   115  calories
     5  grams protein
    17  grams carbohydrate
     1  gram fat
   112  mgs. sodium
     0  mgs. cholesterol
     0  grams dietary fiber

*ADA Exchange Value:*
     1  Starch/Bread
   1/2  Lean meat
    8%  of total calories are from fat.

EUROPEAN CUISINE FROM THE GUILTLESS GOURMET

# Honey Yogurt Cake

> 4  *tablespoons margarine*
> 1/2  *cup honey*
> 6  *egg whites*
> 3/4  *cup plain nonfat yogurt*
> 2  *cups all-purpose flour, sifted*
> 1  *teaspoon baking powder*
> 1/4  *cup finely chopped walnuts*

1. Preheat oven to 350 degrees.
2. Cream margarine and honey together.
3. Add egg whites, 2 at a time, beating after each addition.
4. Fold in yogurt, flour, baking powder, and walnuts.
5. Spoon mixture into loaf pan sprayed with nonstick spray.
6. Bake 1 hour.

Makes 12 servings.

*Each serving contains:*
> 97  *calories*
> 5  *grams protein*
> 17  *grams carbohydrate*
> 1  *gram fat*
> 145  *mgs. sodium*
>   *negligible cholesterol*
> 1  *gram dietary fiber*

*ADA Exchange Value:*
> 1/2  *Starch/Bread*
> 1  *Fruit*
> 9%  *of total calories are from fat.*

# Peach Pudding

3   *1-pound cans water-packed peaches*
2   *envelopes unflavored gelatin*
1   *orange*
2   *packets Equal® sweetener (or 2 teaspoons fructose)*
¹/₂   *cup finely chopped walnuts*

1. Drain peaches, reserving 1 cup liquid.
2. Place gelatin in a bowl.  Heat peach liquid to boiling.  Pour over gelatin.  Stir until dissolved.
3. Juice the orange.  Mix Equal® into juice.
4. Put peaches and orange juice in a food processor with a metal blade or in a blender.  Puree.
5. Add gelatin mixture to puree and mix well.
6. Pour pudding into a mold or bowl and chill until halfway set.
7. Mix walnuts into pudding and let set.
8. To serve, unmold or spoon into small bowls.

Makes 8 servings.

*Each serving contains:*
>    *115   calories*
>      *4   grams protein*
>     *17   grams carbohydrate*
>      *4   grams fat*
>      *7   mgs. sodium*
>      *0   mgs. cholesterol*
>      *2   grams dietary fiber*

*ADA Exchange Value:*
>      *1   Fruit*
>      *1   Fat*
>    *31%   of total calories are from fat.*

# Greek Rice Pudding

  5  cups nonfat milk
  1  cup short-grain white rice
  1  slice of lemon peel, about 1-inch long
 1/2 cup fructose
  3  teaspoons cornstarch
  1  teaspoon vanilla
 1/2 teaspoon almond extract
     Cinnamon

1. Heat milk to boiling.  Add rice and lemon peel.  Lower heat and cook 30 minutes, stirring often.
2. Add fructose and cook 15 minutes more.  Add cornstarch to mixture and cook 5 minutes longer.
3. Remove from heat.  Discard lemon peel.  Stir in vanilla and almond extract.
4. Pour into 8 individual dessert dishes.  Let cool to room temperature.  Sprinkle with cinnamon.

Makes 8 servings.

*Each serving contains:*
      *132  calories*
        *6  grams protein*
       *26  grams carbohydrate*
        *0  grams fat*
       *98  mgs. sodium*
        *0  mgs. cholesterol*
        *0  grams dietary fiber*

*ADA Exchange Value:*
       *1/2  Starch/Bread*
       *3/4  Milk*
       *3/4  Fruit*
            *negligible fat calories.*

# Chicken Broth

1   *3 pound chicken*
3   *stalks celery*
2   *large carrots*
2   *cloves garlic*
$1/4$   *cup fresh parsley, chopped*
1   *large onion*
    *All-purpose herb seasoning*

1. Rinse chicken and place in a crock pot or large pot and cover with water.
2. Peel and chop vegetables into large chunks.  Split garlic cloves in half.
3. Add vegetables, garlic, and parsley to pot.  Sprinkle in about 1 teaspoon herb seasoning.
4. Cover and bring to a boil.  Then simmer several hours.
5. Strain broth into another pot and discard vegetables.
6. Remove skin and bones from chicken.  Shred chicken meat into medium-sized pieces and refrigerate or freeze for use in other recipes.
7. Chill broth for several hours.  Then skim layer of fat from top. Use broth for cooking rice or other dishes needing flavor without adding salt.

Makes about 8 cups.  1 serving = 1 cup

*Each serving contains:*
*10   calories*
*negligible grams protein*
*2   grams carbohydrate*
*negligible fat*
*30   mgs. sodium*
*0   mgs. cholesterol*
*0   grams dietary fiber*

*ADA Exchange Value:*
*Negligible*
*Negligible fat calories.*

# Yogurt Cheese

This is an excellent nonfat replacement for high-fat items—
cream cheese, mayonnaise, or sour cream. You can make it
into a sweet cream or a spicy dip!

**16 oz. plain nonfat yogurt, without any added
gelatin**

1. Place yogurt in a colander lined with coffee filters. Place
   colander with yogurt in a bowl and cover top. Refrigerate for
   18 to 24 hours.
2. Throw out liquid and store Yogurt Cheese in a covered
   container until ready to use.

Makes 8 oz.

*One recipe contains:*
- *225  calories*
- *24  grams protein*
- *32  grams carbohydrate*
- *negligible  fat*
- *150  mgs. sodium*
- *0  mgs. cholesterol*
- *0  grams dietary fiber*

*ADA Exchange Value:*
- *2  Nonfat Milk*
- *Negligible fat calories.*

# Yogurt Cream

This is a no-fat topping that is excellent on top of fruit desserts to give them just that little something extra!

> 1 *cup Yogurt Cheese (page 54)*
> ³/₄ *teaspoon vanilla*
> 4 *packages Equal*™

1. Mix all ingredients together and store in refrigerator in a covered container until ready to use.

Makes 8 servings.

**Each serving contains:**
> 21 *calories*
> 2 *grams protein*
> 2 *grams carbohydrate*
> *negligible fat*
> 20 *mgs. sodium*
> 0 *mgs. cholesterol*
> 0 *grams dietary fiber*

**ADA Exchange Value:**
> **Negligible fat calories.**

# German
# Cuisine

# Germany

The German people are wonderful people who enjoy an exciting cuisine. The northern Germans eat different fare than the Bavarians, but all enjoy potatoes and bread cooked or baked in various ways. Sausages and sauerkraut are common, but we avoided them in this section due to their fat and sodium content. Some specialty companies make delicious lower fat, lower salt versions of these, so look around and you may find some treats to accompany your potato pancakes, spatzle, or dumplings.

Germans are big on celebrations, especially the famous fall Oktoberfest. People from villages, towns, and cities gather to enjoy good food, good music, and lots of beer. Plan your own Oktoberfest party. Put on some oompah music, some polkas, and have a ball.

# Oktoberfest Menu

### Soup

Split Pea Soup

### Main Course

Sauerbraten
Potato Dumplings
Red Cabbage with Apples
Fresh Rye Bread (from your bakery)

### Side Dishes

Cabbage Rolls
Veal Schnitzel

### Dessert

Homemade Applesauce

Serve beer (regular, light, or nonalcoholic.)

Don't forget the music!

# Split Pea Soup

1   *pound bag of split peas, green or yellow*
5   *cups water*
1   *onion, chopped*
2   *carrots, scrubbed and chopped*
$1/2$   *teaspoon marjoram*
$1/2$   *teaspoon thyme*
    *Ground fresh pepper*

1. Rinse peas in a strainer then put into a soup kettle. Add the water and bring to a boil. Skim off any foam that rises to the top. Boil peas for 2 to 3 minutes then cover pot, turn off heat, and let stand for 1 hour.
2. Bring peas back up to a simmer. Add onions, carrots, and herbs. Stir in a few grains of black pepper. Bring to a boil then reduce heat to simmer, covering partially. Simmer for about 1 $1/4$ hours or until peas are soft but not falling apart.

Makes 7 cups. 1 serving = 1 cup

*Each serving contains:*
91   *calories*
6   *grams protein*
17   *grams carbohydrate*
    *negligible grams fat*
10   *mgs. sodium*
0   *mgs. cholesterol*
3   *grams dietary fiber*

*ADA Exchange Value:*
1   *Starch/Bread*
$1/2$   *Vegetable*
    *Negligible fat calories.*

# Chicken and Barley Soup

4  chicken breasts, no skin, bone in
2  quarts cold water
2  carrots, scrubbed and coarsley chopped
2  celery stalks with leaves, coarsley chopped
1  parsnip, scrubbed and coarsley chopped
1  onion, peeled and pierced with whole cloves
   Ground fresh pepper
1/4  cup dried mushrooms, coarsley chopped
1/2  cup boiling water
1/2  cup pearl barley, rinsed
2  tablespoons parsley, finely chopped

1. Combine chicken breasts, water, carrots, celery, parsnip, onion, and a few grindings of fresh pepper in a large pot.
2. Bring to a boil, then reduce to a simmer. Let simmer partially covered for about 30 minutes.
3. In a small bowl, cover the chopped mushrooms with 1/2 cup boiling water and let soak for 30 minutes.
4. Add mushrooms with liquid and barley to soup pot. Stir occasionally and simmer half covered for about one hour or until the barley and mushrooms are tender.
5. Remove chicken breasts from soup. Allow to cool slightly and remove meat from bones. Chop chicken meat coarsley and return to the simmering soup. Discard the onion, stir in parsley and serve.

Makes 6 generous servings.

**Each serving contains:**

| | | |
|---|---|---|
| 179 | calories | **ADA Exchange Value:** |
| 19 | grams protein | 1 Starch/Bread |
| 19 | grams carbohydrate | 2 Lean Meat |
| 3 | grams fat | 1 Vegetable |
| 62 | mgs. sodium | 15% of total |
| 44 | mgs. cholesterol | calories are |
| 3 | grams dietary fiber | from fat. |

# Cabbage Soup with Meatballs

   4   *cups low-salt beef broth*
   $1/2$   *head green cabbage, coarsley chopped*
   3   *carrots, washed and scraped, cut into $1/4$-inch*
       *slices*
   1   *turnip, peeled and cut into small chunks*
   1   *leek, white part only, thinly sliced*
   1   *5 $1/2$-ounce can salt-free vegetable juice*
   $1/2$   *recipe for Swedish Meatballs (page 145)*

1. In a large pot combine beef broth, cabbage, carrots, turnip, leek, and vegetable juice.  Bring to a boil, then reduce heat and simmer.
2. Add Meatballs to simmering pot and heat through.
3. Serve in large soup bowls.  May be served over rice or noodles.

Makes 6 servings.

*Each serving contains:*
   103   *calories*
     9   *grams protein*
    11   *grams carbohydrate*
     3   *grams fat*
   150   *mgs. sodium*
    19   *mgs. cholesterol*
     3   *grams dietary fiber*

*ADA Exchange Value:*
     1   *Lean Meat*
     2   *Vegetable*
   26%   *of total calories are from fat.*

# Hot German Potato Salad

- **4** *medium-size red potatoes, scrubbed but not peeled*
- **2** *tablespoons Butter Buds™, liquid*
- **¹/₂** *cup onion, finely chopped*
- **¹/₄** *cup white vinegar*
- **2** *tablespoons cider vinegar*
- **¹/₄** *cup water*
  *Ground fresh black pepper*
- **2** *tablespoons parsley, finely chopped*
- **¹/₄** *teaspoon celery seed*

1. Boil or steam potatoes until just done; do not overcoo. Drain.
2. Allow potatoes to cool slightly, then slice into ¹/₄-inch slices into a large serving bowl.
3. Heat Butter Buds™ in a nonstick pan and add onions. Cook just until soft and transparent. Stir in the vinegar, water, pepper, and celery seed. Stir and cook for about 2 minutes more. Pour the sauce over the hot potatoes. Stir gently and serve.

Makes 6 servings.

*Each serving contains:*
- **85** *calories*
- **2** *grams protein*
- **20** *grams carbohydrate*
  *negligible grams fat*
- **20** *mgs. sodium*
- **0** *mgs. cholesterol*
- **1** *gram dietary fiber*

*ADA Exchange Value:*
- **1** *Starch/Bread*
  *Negligible fat calories.*

# Leek Salad

**6  firm, fresh leeks, 1 to 1 ¹/₂ inches in diameter**
**¹/₄  cup low-calorie sour cream**
**¹/₄  cup cider vinegar**
**1  teaspoon German-style mustard**
**1  teaspoon bottled horseradish**
**Ground fresh black pepper**
**Lettuce**
**Pickled beets for garnish**

1. To prepare leeks, cut the roots off and strip away any old, outer leaves.  Line up the leeks in a row and cut off enough of the green top so that each leek is 6 to 7 inches long.  Rinse very well to remove any fine sand.
2. Lay leeks flat in a steamer and steam 3 to 5 minutes or until they show a slight resistance when pierced with a fork.  Do not overcook.
3. Drain leeks well, reserving ¹/₄ cup of liquid.  Arrange leeks in a serving dish or deep platter.
4. Combine cooking liquid with sour cream, vinegar, mustard, horseradish, and pepper.  Mix well and pour over leeks and chill.
5. To serve, arrange leeks on a bed of lettuce.  Garnish with pickled beets.

Makes 6 servings.

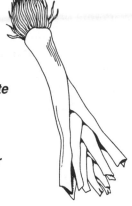

*Each serving contains:*
  *38  calories*
   *2  grams protein*
   *5  grams carbohydrate*
   *2  grams fat*
   *9  mgs. sodium*
   *4  mgs. cholesterol*
   *2  grams dietary fiber*

*ADA Exchange Value:*
   *1  Vegetable*
  *47%  of total calories are from fat.*

# Garlic Vegetable Medley

$1/4$   cup Chicken Broth (page 53)
   1   clove garlic, minced
$1/2$   head fresh cauliflower, steamed
   1   large zucchini, sliced and steamed
   2   carrots, scrubbed and steamed
   2   tablespoons Parmesan cheese

1. Spray a skilled with nonstick spray. Heat skillet to medium hot and add minced garlic. Cook, stirring often, until garlic just begins to brown.
2. Add Chicken Broth to skillet, then add the steamed vegetables.
3. Cover pan and let vegetables cook just long enough to heat through. Remove cover and sprinkle on Parmesan cheese. Cover again, just long enough to melt cheese. Serve.

Makes 4 servings. 1 serving = approx. 1 cup

Each serving contains:
   44   calories
    3   grams protein
   10   grams carbohydrate
        negligible grams fat
   40   mgs. sodium
        negligible mg. cholesterol
    4   grams dietary fiber

ADA Exchange Value:
    2   Vegetable
        Negligible fat calories.

# Red Cabbage with Apples

*Small head of red cabbage*
2/3 *cup red wine vinegar*
2 *tablespoons fructose*
2 *tablespoons Butter Buds™, liquid*
2 *medium cooking apples, cored and cut into chunks*
1/2 *cup onion, finely chopped*
1 *whole onion, peeled and pierced with 2 whole cloves*
1 *bay leaf*
1 *cup boiling water*
3 *tablespoons dry red wine (optional)*

1. Wash the cabbage well and remove any tough outer leaves. Cut cabbage into quarters. Shred the cabbage into 1/8 inch-wide strips by hand or using a food processor.
2. Place the cabbage into a large mixing bowl. Add vinegar and fructose and toss evenly to coat the shreds.
3. In a heavy casserole heat Butter Buds™, adding apples and chopped onion. Cook, stirring frequently, for 5 minutes or until the apples are lightly browned.
4. Add the cabbage, the whole onion with cloves, the bay leaf, and boiling water to the casserole. Stir to mix well. Bring all to a boil, then cover, reduce to a simmer, and cook for 1 1/2 to 2 hours. Check occasionally to see if cabbage is too dry; if so, add a little hot water. When the cabbage is done there should be almost no liquid left in the casserole.
5. Remove the whole onion and the bay leaf. Stir in wine, if desired. Serve.

Makes 8 servings. 1 serving = 1/2 cup

*Each serving contains:*
- *49 calories*
- *1 gram protein*
- *12 grams carbohydrate*
  - *negligible grams fat*
- *19 mgs. sodium*
- *0 mgs. cholesterol*
- *2 grams dietary fiber*

*ADA Exchange Value:*
- *1 Vegetable*
- *1/2 Fruit*
  - *negligible fat calories.*

# Green Beans with Lettuce

½ **pound fresh green beans, ends snapped and cut in half**

1 **small onion, chopped**

½ **cup + 2 tablespoons Chicken Broth (page 53)**

½ **head lettuce**

¼ **teaspoon marjoram**

⅛ **teaspoon dill**

1 **tablespoon Butter Buds™, dry**

1 **tablespoon flour**

1. Steam green beans until almost tender, yet slightly crisp (do not overcook).
2. Spray a skillet with nonstick spray, heat to medium hot, and saute onion until soft. Add partially cooked green beans and ½ cup of chicken broth.
3. Add lettuce, marjoram, and dill. Stir to mix. Cover and cook about 2 minutes.
4. Mix together Butter Buds™ and flour, then stir in 2 tablespoons of Broth. Stir until smooth.
5. Remove lid from pan and tip the pan slightly to allow juices to run to one side. Add the flour mixture to the juices and stir until thickened. Mix thickened juices into vegetables in pan. Cover and cook about 1 minute more.

Makes 4 servings. 1 serving = approximately ¾ cup

*Each serving contains:*
- 35 *calories*
- 2 *grams protein*
- 7 *grams carbohydrate*
- *negligible grams fat*
- 20 *mgs. sodium*
- *negligible cholesterol*
- 2 *grams dietary fiber*

*ADA Exchange Value:*
- 1 *Vegetable*
- *Negligible fat calories.*

# Dilled Carrots in Beer

1    *tablespoon fructose*
1/4  *cup beer*
1/4  *teaspoon dill*
1/2  *pound carrots, scrubbed, sliced, and steamed*

1. Place fructose in the bottom of a heavy saucepan. Allow to melt slowly over medium heat, stirring constantly. Watch carefully until it just begins to carmelize or turn a light brown color.
2. Carefully add beer to the pan. Stir in dill and cooked carrots. Stir to coat carrots and heat through.

Makes 4 servings.  1 serving = approximately 1/2 cup

*Each serving contains:*
   28   *calories*
    1   *gram protein*
    6   *grams carbohydrate*
    0   *grams fat*
   29   *mgs. sodium*
    0   *mgs. cholesterol*
    1   *gram dietary fiber*

       *ADA Exchange Value*
    1   *Vegetable*
       *negligible fat calories.*

# Colcannon

A great way to use up leftovers!

- 1   onion, minced
- 1/2   cup nonfat milk
- 2   medium potatoes, boiled
- 2   parsnips, boiled
- 2   tablespoons Butter Buds™, liquid
  Ground fresh pepper
- 1   cup cabbage, shredded and cooked
- 1   tablespoon parsley, minced

1. Cook onions in milk until tender.
2. Mash potatoes and parsnips together; season with Butter Buds™ and pepper.  Add onions and milk slowly, beating well.
3. Stir in cabbage and garnish with parsley.

Makes 8 servings.

*Each serving contains:*
- 65   *calories*
- 2   *grams protein*
- 15   *grams carbohydrate*
  *negligible grams fat*
- 65   *mgs. sodium*
  *negligible mg. cholesterol*
- 2   *grams dietary fiber*

*ADA Exchange Value:*
- 1/2   *Starch/Bread*
- 1   *Vegetable*
  *Negligible fat calories.*

# Scalloped Turnips and Potatoes

2 medium turnips, peeled
2 medium potatoes, peeled
2 tablespoons Butter Buds™, liquid
Ground fresh pepper
$^1/_2$ cup reduced-calorie sour cream
$^1/_4$ cup nonfat milk
2 green onions, minced
Chopped parsley

1. Preheat oven to 350 degrees.
2. Slice turnips and potatoes in $^1/_8$-inch rounds and arrange in a baking dish that has been sprayed with nonstick spray.
3. Drizzle Butter Buds™ over top.
4. Mix pepper with sour cream, milk, and green onion. Pour over potato-turnip mixture.
5. Cover casserole and bake for 45 minutes to 1 hour. Remove cover when $^3/_4$ done cooking to allow for browning. Garnish with parsley.

Makes 6 servings.

*Each serving contains:*
90 *calories*
3 *grams protein*
16 *grams carbohydrate*
2 *grams fat*
58 *mgs. sodium*
4 *mgs. cholesterol*
3 *grams dietary fiber*

*ADA Exchange Value:*
1 *Starch/Bread*
20% *of total calories are from fat.*

# Potato Pancakes

These are good as a side dish or served with applesauce (see page 92)

> 2 *medium-size baking potatoes*
> 2 *egg whites*
> 1/4 *cup onion, finely grated*
> 1/4 *cup flour*

1. Peel potatoes, dropping each one into a bowl of cold water to prevent discoloring.
2. In a large mixing bowl, beat the egg whites. Add onion and gradually beat in the flour.
3. Using one potato at a time, pat the potato dry and grate coarsely into a sieve or colander. Press each potato down firmly into the sieve in order to squeeze out as much moisture as possible. Add immediately to egg and onion batter.
4. Preheat oven to 250 degrees. Spray nonstick spray into a heavy skillet, heat until very hot, then pour 1/4 cup of the potato mixture into skillet. Flatten mixture with a spatula into a pancake about 5 inches in diameter. Cook for about 2 minutes on each side.
5. When pancake is golden brown and crisp around the edges, transfer to an ovenproof dish and keep in the warm oven.
6. Continue making pancakes as described, adding a little more nonstick spray to the skillet as needed and allowing it to heat before adding more batter.

Makes 4 servings. 1 serving = 2 pancakes

*Each serving contains:*
- 55 *calories*
- 2 *grams protein*
- 12 *grams carbohydrate*
- 0 *grams fat*
- 15 *mgs. sodium*
- 0 *mgs. cholesterol*
- 1 *gram dietary fiber*

*ADA Exchange Value*
*3/4 Starch/Bread*
*Negligible fat calories.*

# Potato Dumplings

²/₃ **cup mashed potato**

1 **cup flour**

4 **teaspoons baking powder**

2 **teaspoons oil**

¹/₂ **cup milk, (plus or minus 1 to 2 tablespoons)**

1. Combine all ingredients into a dough.  Roll out dough to about ¹/₂-inch thick.
2. Cut into 12 biscuit-shaped pieces using a 2-inch biscuit cutter.
3. Spray a large steamer basket with nonstick spray and place over boiling water.  Carefully lay dumplings into steamer basket.
4. Cover and steam about 12 minutes or until done.

Makes 12 dumplings.  1 serving = 1 dumpling

**Each serving contains:**

     *59 calories*

      *2 grams protein*

   *10 grams carbohydrate*

      *1 gram fat*

 *171 mgs. sodium*

        *negligible mg. cholesterol*

      *1 gram dietary fiber*

      *ADA Exchange Value*

³/₄ *Starch/Bread*

*15% of total calories are from fat.*

# Spatzle

1 1/2  cups all-purpose flour
  1/4  teaspoon ground nutmeg
    1  whole egg
    2  egg whites
  1/2  cup nonfat milk

1. In a mixing bowl, combine flour and nutmeg.
2. Beat whole egg and whites together, then pour into flour mixture and stir to mix well. Pour milk in using a thin stream and stirring constantly with a large spoon. Stir until dough is smooth.
3. Bring 2 quarts of water to a boil. Set a large colander, one with large holes, over the pot. Pour dough into colander a little at a time, pressing the dough through the holes and directly into the water.
4. When all dough has dropped into water, remove colander. Stir dumplings gently to prevent them from sticking. Boil briskly for 5 to 8 minutes or until tender. Remove from water with a slotted spoon. Serve as a side dish or accompaniment to other German dishes.

Makes 6 servings.

*Each serving contains:*
       119  *calories*
         6  *grams protein*
        23  *grams carbohydrate*
            *negligible grams fat*
        39  *mgs. sodium*
            *negligible mg. cholesterol*
         1  *gram dietary fiber*

*ADA Exchange Value:*
    1 1/2  *Starch/Bread*
            *negligible fat calories.*

# German Chicken

4 chicken breasts, skin removed, bone in
  Paprika
1 small head green cabbage, cored and cut into
  1/2-inch wedges
1 medium onion, sliced
2 cooking apples, cored and sliced into rings
2 teaspoons caraway seeds
1/2 cup reduced-calorie sour cream
1 tablespoon flour

1. Preheat oven to 350 degrees.
2. Spray an oven-proof skillet with nonstick spray. Sprinkle chicken breasts with paprika and brown on both sides in heated skillet. Remove chicken to a platter.
3. Add cabbage, onion, apple, and caraway seeds to skillet and cook several minutes until vegetables are softened but not fully cooked. Place chicken breasts on top of cabbage mixture, cover, and bake for 45 minutes. Remove from oven.
4. Combine flour with sour cream. Remove chicken to a warm platter, stir sour cream mixture slowly into vegetables and juices. Heat gently if needed to thicken slightly. Serve on a plate with chicken breasts on top.

Makes 4 servings.

**Each serving contains:**
224 calories
27 grams protein
18 grams carbohydrate
5 grams fat
80 mgs. sodium
79 mgs. cholesterol
4 grams dietary fiber

**ADA Exchange Value:**
3 Lean Meat
2 Vegetable
1/2 Fruit
20% of total calories are from fat.

EUROPEAN CUISINE FROM THE GUILTLESS GOURMET

# Hungarian Noodle Bake

  4   ounces noodles, dry
  1   cup nonfat cottage cheese
 1/2  cup reduced-calorie sour cream
 1/2  cup nonfat yogurt
 1/4  cup onion, finely chopped
  1   clove garlic, minced
 1/2  teaspoon cayenne pepper
  1   tablespoon poppy seeds
      Ground fresh pepper
      Paprika
  2   tablespoons Parmesan cheese

1. Preheat oven to 350 degrees.  Cook noodles in boiling water until just tender.  Drain.
2. Combine cottage cheese, sour cream, yogurt, onion, garlic, cayenne pepper, and poppy seeds.  Stir to mix and add a few grinds of black pepper.
3. Mix noodles with cottage cheese mixture.  Pour into a square baking dish, sprinkle with paprika, and bake uncovered for 25 to 30 minutes.  Just before removing from the oven, sprinkle with Parmesan cheese.  Serve.

Makes 6 servings.

*Each serving contains:*
    115   *calories*
     10   *grams protein*
     17   *grams carbohydrate*
      1   *gram fat*
    209   *mgs. sodium*
      3   *mgs. cholesterol*
      1   *gram dietary fiber*

*ADA Exchange Value:*
      1   *Lean Meat*
      1   *Starch/Bread*
     8%   *of total calories are from fat.*

# Chicken Paprikash

1   pound chicken fillets, boned and skinned
2   tablespoons Butter Buds™, liquid
1   onion, finely chopped
1   tablespoon paprika
1 ½   cups Chicken Broth (see page 53)
1   tablespoon flour
1   cup reduced-calorie sour cream
2   cups rice, cooked

1. Spray a heavy skillet with nonstick spray. Begin to saute the onions, adding Butter Buds™ liquid gradually. Cook and stir until onions are cooked and all Butter Buds™ are used. Stir in paprika.
2. Slowly add chicken broth and heat to a boil. Immediately reduce heat to a simmer, add chicken breasts, cover, and simmer gently for about 20 minutes or until chicken is cooked through.
3. Mix flour with sour cream. Stir slowly into chicken mixture, never allowing it to boil. Stir until slightly thickened. Serve over cooked rice.

Makes 4 servings.

*Each serving contains:*
  331   calories
   30   grams protein
   34   grams carbohydrate
    8   grams fat
  204   mgs. sodium
   45   mgs. cholesterol
    1   gram dietary fiber

*ADA Exchange Value:*
    3   Lean Meat
    2   Starch/Bread
  22%   of total calories are from fat.

# Cabbage Rolls

1   head cabbage
1   pound extra lean ground beef (or any lean
    ground meat)
1/2   cup onion, finely chopped
1   teaspoon thyme
1   clove garlic, minced
    Dash of cayenne pepper
1/2   cup reduced-salt beef stock, boiling

*Sauce:*

4   fresh tomatoes, diced
1/4   cup onion, finely chopped
1/2   teaspoon thyme
1/4   cup carrot, grated (1 small carrot)

1. In a large pot bring several cups of water to a boil. Remove
   stem portion from head of cabbage and drop entire head into
   boiling water for a few seconds. Carefully remove one leaf at
   a time. When you have removed 8 leaves, take rest of
   cabbage out of water. Return the 8 leaves to boiling water
   and blanch for about 2 minutes.
2. Remove leaves, drain, and plunge into cold water to stop the
   cooking process. When cooled, set leaves aside to drain.
3. Preheat oven to 350 degrees.
4. Combine ground beef with onion, parsley, thyme, garlic, and
   cayenne pepper. Mix well; then divide into 8 equal parts.
5. Place a cooked cabbage leaf on a flat surface. Place one
   portion of raw meat mixture in center and fold up bottom part,
   fold over sides and top to make a neat package. Continue
   with rest of leaves and meat mixture.
6. Place cabbage rolls into a heat-proof casserole. Pour boiling
   broth over the rolls and cover. Bake 50 to 60 minutes.
7. Prepare sauce while rolls are baking. Combine sauce
   ingredients in a skillet sprayed with nonstick spray, cover, and
   let cook slowly for most of the time rolls are in the oven. For
   the last 10 minutes of baking, add sauce to rolls, cover, and
   finish baking. Serve.

Makes 4 servings.  1 serving = 2 rolls

*Each serving contains:*
- *167 calories*
- *20 grams protein*
- *9 grams carbohydrate*
- *6 grams fat*
- *217 mgs. sodium*
- *52 mgs. cholesterol*
- *3 grams dietary fiber*

*ADA Exchange Value:*
- *2 Lean Meat*
- *1 Vegetable*
- *32% of total calories are from fat.*

# Whitefish and Potatoes

    4   medium or 8 small red potatoes, scrubbed but
        not peeled
1 ¹/₂   pounds firm, fresh whitefish fillets
        Juice of one lemon
   ¹/₄   cup Butter Buds™, liquid
    1   cup onion, finely chopped
    3   tablespoons German-style or hot prepared
        mustard
        Parsley, chopped or green onion tops, minced

1. Preheat oven to 350 degrees.
2. Place potatoes in enough water to cover. Boil until just cooked (do not overcook).
3. Rinse fish fillets under running water and pat dry with paper towels. Sprinkle both sides with lemon juice and let rest for 10 minutes.
4. Dip fillets into 2 tablespoons liquid Butter Buds™, turning to coat thoroughly. Arrange side by side in a baking dish. Sprinkle chopped onions on top and bake in oven for 12 to 15 minutes or until firm and opaque.
5. Heat a deep serving platter. Drain and cool potatoes slightly, then slice crosswise into ¹/₄-inch thick rounds. Arrange potato slices, overlapping in a circular manner on heated serving platter.
6. Place baked fish on top of potatoes. Mix remaining liquid from fish with about 2 tablespoons Butter Buds™ and mustard. Heat quickly and pour over top of fish and potatoes. Garnish with parsley or green onions. Serve immediately.

Makes 6 servings.

*Each serving contains:*
- *216 calories*
- *29 grams protein*
- *22 grams carbohydrate*
- *1 gram fat*
- *162 mgs. sodium*
- *64 mgs. cholesterol*
- *2 grams dietary fiber*

*ADA Exchange Value:*
- *3 Lean Meat*
- *1 1/2 Starch/Bread*
- *4% of total calories are from fat.*

# Veal Schnitzel

There are many variations for schnitzel. Usually breading and frying is the first step. This version gives a similar taste and appearance without the added fat.

> 1 *medium onion, thinly sliced*
> 1 *clove garlic, minced*
> 1 *pound veal cutlets (scallopini cut)*
> 1 to 2 *teaspoons paprika*
> 2 *tablespoons flour*

1. Spray a skillet with nonstick spray and heat to a medium temperature. Saute onions and garlic until soft.
2. Combine paprika and flour. Sprinkle over veal cutlets and pound cutlets with the edge of a plate or a cleaver.
3. Add cutlets to pan with onions and garlic. Reduce heat slightly if necessary and brown cutlets well on both sides. Cutlets cook quickly. Serve on a plate with onion and garlic mixture on top.

Makes 4 servings.

*Each serving contains:*
> 255 *calories*
> 30 *grams protein*
> 5 *grams carbohydrate*
> 12 *grams fat*
> 71 *mgs. sodium*
> 108 *mgs. cholesterol*
> 1 *gram dietary fiber*

*ADA Exchange Value:*
> 4 *Lean Meat*
> 1 *Vegetable*
> 18% *of total calories are from fat.*

# Pork Chops with Potatoes

4   lean loin chops, trimmed, 4 to 5 ounces raw
      with bone
4   small to medium potatoes, scrubbed and sliced
      White Sauce (page 104)
¼   cup vermouth

1. Preheat oven to 350 degrees.
2. Make White Sauce according to directions, adding vermouth
   at the end.  Stir to mix well and set aside.
3. Spray a heavy skillet with nonstick spray.  Brown chops on
   both sides, then layer sliced potatoes on top.  Pour White
   Sauce over potatoes.  Cover and bake for 1 to 1 ½ hours.

Makes 4 servings.  1 serving = 1 pork chop and 1 potato

*Each serving contains:*
- 224  *calories*
- 14  *grams protein*
- 33  *grams carbohydrate*
- 3  *grams fat*
- 111  *mgs. sodium*
- 28  *mgs. cholesterol*
- 2  *grams dietary fiber*

*ADA Exchange Value:*
- 2  *Lean Meat*
- 2  *Starch/Bread*
- 12%  *of total calories are from fat.*

# Fruited Pork Tenderloin

1 1/2  *pounds pork tenderloin*
   1  *apple, cored and cut into rings*
   8  *dried prunes*
   8  *dried apricot halves*
   1  *teaspoon rosemary or sprig of fresh rosemary*
 1/4  *cup dry white wine (optional)*
    *Plastic cooking bag*

1. Preheat oven to 325 degrees.
2. Remove tenderloin from package, rinse, and pat dry. Follow package directions for preparing plastic cooking bag. Place pork in bag and put into a medium-size roasting pan.
3. Place apple slices, prunes, and apricots decoratively onto pork. Sprinkle rosemary on top. Add wine if desired. Secure bag and roast for about 1 1/2 hours or until 185 degrees internal temperature.
4. Carefully remove pork and fruit from bag and set onto a platter. Carve into thin slices and serve.

Makes 24 slices. 1 serving = 3 slices

**Each serving contains:**
   270  *calories*
    28  *grams protein*
    10  *grams carbohydrate*
    12  *grams fat*
    63  *mgs. sodium*
    90  *mgs. cholesterol*
     2  *grams dietary fiber*

**ADA Exchange Value:**
    4  *Lean Meat*
 1/2  *Fruit*
 40%  *of total calories are from fat.*

# Mock Short Ribs with Caper Sauce

 2 pounds center cut beef shanks, round bone in
   Freshly ground black pepper
 2 medium onions, sliced 1/8-inch thick
 1 bay leaf
 1/4 teaspoon ground cloves
 4 cups cold water
 1 slice fresh dark rye bread, made into crumbs
 2 teaspoons capers, drained and rinsed
 2 tablespoons lemon juice
 1/2 teaspoon lemon peel, finely grated

1. Sprinkle beef shanks with pepper. Spray a Dutch oven with nonstick spray. Heat Dutch oven, add beef shanks, and brown on both sides. Remove to a platter.
2. Add onions to the Dutch oven. Cook over low to medium heat until they are transparent but not brown. Add the bay leaf, cloves, and water. Bring to a boil.
3. Return shanks to the pot, cover, and reduce heat to low. Simmer for 1 1/2 hours or until meat is very tender.
4. Heat a platter. Transfer meat to platter and cover with foil to keep warm. Discard the bay leaf and skim any fat from the remaining liquid.
5. Stir bread crumbs, capers, lemon juice, and lemon peel into liquid. Bring to a boil, reduce heat, and simmer for a minute or two.
6. Pour sauce over meat and serve at once in large soup plates. Sauce should be quite peppery.

Makes 6 servings.

*Each serving contains:*
- *186  calories*
- *22  grams protein*
- *5  grams carbohydrate*
- *8  grams fat*
- *77  mgs. sodium*
- *78  mgs. cholesterol*
- *1  gram dietary fiber*

*ADA Exchange Value:*
- *3  Lean Meat*
- *1  Vegetable*
- *39%  of total calories are from fat.*

# Beef Rouladen

1 1/2   **pounds top round steak, sliced 1/2-inch thick, trimmed and pounded to 1/4 inch thick**
  6   **teaspoons German-style mustard**
  1/4   **cup onion, finely chopped**
      **Celery stalks**
  2   **cups water**
  1   **cup celery, coarsely chopped**
  1/4   **cup leeks, white part only, thinly sliced**
  1   **parsnip, small, scraped, finely chopped**
  3   **sprigs parsley**
  2   **tablespoons Butter Buds™, dry**
  2   **tablespoons flour**

1. Cut the pounded meat into rectangular pieces about 4 inches wide and 8 inches long. Spread each rectangle with mustard, sprinkle with onion, and lay a strip of celery across the narrow end of each piece.
2. Roll each piece jelly-roll style into a cylinder. Secure each roll by piercing with skewer or a toothpick or by tying with a piece of twine.
3. Spray a heavy skillet with nonstick spray, and heat to a moderate heat. Add beef rolls and brown on all sides slowly so as not to burn them. Transfer the rolls to a plate.
4. Pour water into the skillet and bring to a boil. Add celery, leeks, parsnip, and parsley, and return beef to the skillet.
5. Cover skillet and reduce heat. Simmer for one hour or until the meat seems very tender. Turn the rolls once or twice during the cooking period. Heat a platter. Transfer the rolls to heated platter and cover while making sauce.
6. Strain the cooking liquid through a fine sieve, pressing hard on the vegetables before discarding them. Measure the liquid, return to skillet and boil briskly until it is reduced to 2 cups. Remove from heat.
7. In a small bowl mix Butter Buds™ and flour thoroughly. Add 1/4 cup of cooking liquid and mix well to avoid lumps. Gradually add the mixture to the hot liquid, stirring with a whisk until the sauce is smooth and thick. Strain if necessary.
8. Return the sauce and Rouladen to the skillet. Simmer over low heat just long enough for the rolls to heat through.

Makes 6 servings.

*Each serving contains:*
>    198  calories
>      26  grams protein
>        5  grams carbohydrate
>        8  grams fat
>    167  mgs. sodium
>      72  mgs. cholesterol
>        1  gram dietary fiber

*ADA Exchange Value:*
>        3  Lean Meat
>        1  Vegetable
>    36%  of total calories are from fat.

# Sauerbraten

This is a traditional recipe often served for special occasions. It requires 2 to 3 days to marinate and about 2 hours to cook. It is delicious served with dumplings or boiled potatoes and red cabbage.

2   *pounds lean rump roast, trimmed of any fat*
1/2   *cup red wine vinegar*
1/2   *cup cider vinegar*
1   *medium onion, sliced thin*
   *Freshly ground black pepper*
1   *bay leaf*
1/2   *teaspoon ground allspice*
4   *whole cloves*
1   *carrot, scrubbed and sliced*
1   *stalk celery, sliced*
6   *gingersnaps, crushed*

1. In a glass or ceramic bowl, combine vinegars, onion, several grinds of pepper, bay leaf, allspice, cloves, carrot, and celery.
2. Rinse roast, pat dry, and add to marinade. Cover tightly and refrigerate for 2 to 3 days, turning once or twice a day.
3. Remove meat and pat dry. Strain marinade and reserve. Heat a Dutch oven or heavy kettle that has been sprayed with nonstick spray. Add roast and brown on all sides.
4. Pour in reserved marinade and simmer, covered, for about 2 hours or until roast is tender.
5. Remove roast to heated platter. Remove any fat from liquid in Dutch oven. Bring liquid to a boil.
6. Add gingersnap crumbs to liquid and gently boil about 5 minutes until liquid is slightly thickened.
7. To serve, slice meat very thin and place on individual plates or a serving platter. Ladle sauce on top.

Makes 6 servings. 1 serving = 3 slices

*Each serving contains:*
- *281 calories*
- *35 grams protein*
- *10 grams carbohydrate*
- *11 grams fat*
- *115 mgs. sodium*
- *99 mgs. cholesterol*
- *1 gram dietary fiber*

*ADA Exchange Value:*
- *4 Lean Meat*
- *1 Vegetable*
- *1/2 Starch/Bread*
- *35% of total calories are from fat.*

# Carrot Bread

- ¹/₂ **cup fructose**
- 2 **tablespoons molasses**
- ¹/₄ **cup oil**
- ¹/₂ **cup nonfat yogurt, plain**
- 4 **egg whites**
- 1 **teaspoon vanilla**
- 1 **cup whole wheat flour, sifted**
- 1 **cup unbleached flour, sifted**
- 1 ¹/₂ **teaspoons baking powder**
- 1 **teaspoon baking soda**
- 1 **teaspoon cinnamon**
- 1 **cup carrots, grated**

1. Preheat oven to 350 degrees. Spray a 9 x 5 x 2 ¹/₂-inch bread pan with nonstick spray.
2. In a medium-size bowl combine fructose, molasses, oil, yogurt, vanilla, and egg whites. Stir to mix well, then stir in grated carrots.
3. In a separate bowl sift flours with baking powder, soda, and cinnamon. Add flour to carrot mixture a little at a time, stirring to mix. Do not beat or overstir.
4. Pour batter into bread pan. Bake in oven 50 to 60 minutes or until done. Cool on a rack, removing from pan as soon as cool enough to handle.

Makes 18 servings. 1 serving = 1 slice

**Each serving contains:**
- 84 *calories*
- 3 *grams protein*
- 16 *grams carbohydrate*
- 1 *gram fat*
- 129 *mgs. sodium*
- 0 *mgs. cholesterol*
- 1 *gram dietary fiber*

**ADA Exchange Value:**
- 1 *Starch/Bread*
- 11% *of total calories are from fat.*

# Homemade Applesauce

*6  medium cooking apples, with peel*
*1  tablespoon fructose (if desired)*

1. Wash apples, core, quarter, and cut into bite-size pieces.  Put apples into a medium-size saucepan.  Add about 2 tablespoons water.  Bring to a boil, then reduce heat, cover, and cook about 20 minutes or until apples are very done.  Check occasionally to be sure they have enough liquid.
2. Cool slightly.  Add fructose if extra sweetness is desired.

Makes 8 servings.

*Each serving contains:*
*65  calories*
    *negligible grams protein*
*17  grams carbohydrate*
    *Negligible grams fat*
 *2  mgs. sodium*
 *0  mgs. cholesterol*
 *3  grams dietary fiber*

*ADA Exchange Value:*
 *1  Fruit*
    *Negligible fat calories.*

# English
# Cuisine

# England

## High Tea

In England High Tea is served between 3 and 5 o'clock in the afternoon. It's great fun, so why not plan a High Tea for your next get-together, whether it's a wedding, baby shower, or just for fun. Use your best dishes and have fun with the little touches like flowers and classical music to add to the atmosphere.

# Menu

Tea
Milk or lemon

Variety of tea sandwiches

Crumpet Scones and Fruit Scones
Sugar-Free Jam and Yogurt Cream

Chocolate-Filled Sponge Cake
Sherry Trifle

# English Cuisine

London is our favorite city. Its history, art, and cab drivers are not to be matched anywhere. We have made several trips to this great city and have explored the English countryside.

Americans tend to think that English food is boring. We totally disagree, and we are sure this segment of *European Cuisine from the Guiltless Gourmet* will change your mind. English people do things with ceremony and tradition.

In London most people live in small flats with tiny kitchens that don't have much storage space, which means that most people shop daily for their evening meal and buy in small portions. Many people do their entertaining at the local pub. On the contrary, if you travel out of London to the countryside, you find large homes with magnificent kitchens!

One of the English traditions we like the most is High Tea, usually served from 3 to 5 o'clock in the afternoon. We decided we wanted to include a segment on English teas in one of our books. We hope you will enjoy putting on your own tea using the Guiltless methods to cut fat calories out of high-fat foods.

English cooking is also called white cooking because it uses very few spices, and the most frequently used sauce is the white sauce. We have modified the white sauce to make it very low in calories. Most meats are roasted, which is also easy to modify. We will move on to the English kitchen and plan a High Tea.

## English Tea

Tea is one of the English traditions we truly enjoy. Teahas become more popular in the United States in the last few years. If you have not experienced a good cup of tea, well, it's time you did.

You can find several good quality teas in bags, which work well if you're on the run or want to keep some in the office. However, for a truly good pot of tea, it's best to steep it with loose tea leaves. Start with a glass or china teapot and fill it with boiling water. Let it stand a couple of minutes, then pour out the water. Spoon 1 teaspoon of loose tea per cup into the pot, then pour boiling water over the tea. Let it steep 3 to 5 minutes (time will be stated on your tea tin). Pour the tea through a tea strainer into a cup. Serve with lemon wedges or milk (never cream) and the sweetener of your choice.

If you find you enjoy tea, keep a lookout for special teapots and cups you might like to serve your friends with. To find the teas that you like best, go to a coffee shop that also specializes in tea and talk to the proprietors. They can help you select the tea best suited to your taste.

## Tea Sandwiches

Sandwiches for tea are always very light and delicate. Listed here are several choices. Each recipe will make eight sand-wiches. For tea you want to cut off the crust and slice in thirds (strips) or cut in 4 triangles. You can also make a hardier sandwich from these recipes by using more filling and not cutting off the crust. Make the sandwiches as close to serving time as possible, then cover with a damp cloth.

# Basic Sandwich Spread

1  *cup yogurt cheese*
2  *tablespoons mustard*

1. Mix together, and use 1 teaspoon on each slice of bread for making sandwiches.

1 serving = 1 teaspoon

*Each serving contains:*
   *3  calories*
   *0.3  grams protein*
   *0.4  grams carbohydrate*
   *0.1  gram fat*
   *6  mgs. sodium*
   *0  mgs. cholesterol*
   *0  dietary fiber*

   *ADA Exchange Value*
   *Negligible fat calories.*

# Egg and Watercress Sandwiches

>    1  cup watercress, washed, patted dry, and
>       chopped
>    5  hard-boiled eggs, shelled and chopped
>    5  tablespoons yogurt cheese
> 2 1/2  tablespoons Dijon mustard
>       White pepper to taste
>   16  slices extra-thin wheat bread

1. Mix all ingredients together well.
2. Make sandwiches, cut off crust, cut sandwiches, and cover.

Makes 8 sandwiches.  1 serving = 1 sandwich

*Each serving contains:*
>    93  *calories*
>     7  *grams protein*
>    12  *grams carbohydrate*
>     2  *grams fat*
>   234  *mgs. sodium*
>   173  *mgs. cholesterol*
>     3  *grams dietary fiber*

*ADA Exchange Value:*
>     1  *Starch/Bread*
>   1/2  *Lean Meat*
>   19%  *of total calories are from fat.*

# Tuna Sandwiches

1  7-ounce can water-packed tuna, drained and flaked
5  tablespoons low-calorie mayonnaise
1  tablespoon Dijon mustard
1  teaspoon sweet pickle relish
16  slices extra-thin wheat bread

1. Mix all ingredients together and let stand at least 2 hours in the refrigerator.
2. Make sandwiches, cut off crusts, cut sandwiches, and cover.

Makes 8 sandwiches. 1 serving = 1 sandwich

*Each serving contains:*
113  calories
9  grams protein
12  grams carbohydrate
4  grams fat
270  mgs. sodium
13  mgs. cholesterol
3  grams dietary fiber

*ADA Exchange Value:*
1  Lean Meat
1  Starch/Bread
32%  of total calories are from fat.

# Yogurt Cream, Celery, and Walnut Sandwiches

2   *cups yogurt cream*
2   *cups chopped celery*
$^1/_2$   *cup chopped walnuts*
16   *slices extra-thin wheat bread*

1. Mix ingredients together.
2. Make sandwiches, cut off crusts, cut sandwiches, and cover.

Makes 8 sandwiches.  1 serving = 1 sandwich

*Each serving contains:*

144   *calories*
7   *grams protein*
17   *grams carbohydrate*
1   *gram fat*
187   *mgs. sodium*
4   *mgs. cholesterol*
4   *grams dietary fiber*

*ADA Exchange Value:*

1   *Lean Meat*
1   *Starch/Bread*
1   *Fruit*
6%   *of total calories are from fat.*

# Chicken Sandwiches

8 ounces skinless chicken breast, sliced and cooked
16 teaspoons Sandwich Spread (page 96)
16 slices extra-thin wheat bread

1. Spread 1 teaspoon of spread on each slice of bread. Place 1 ounce of chicken in each sandwich. Cut off crusts, cut sandwiches, and cover.

Makes 8 sandwiches. 1 serving = 1 sandwich

*Each serving contains:*
107 calories
11 grams protein
12 grams carbohydrate
2 grams fat
145 mgs. sodium
23 mgs. cholesterol
3 grams dietary fiber

*ADA Exchange Value:*
1 Lean Meat
1 Starch/Bread
17% of total calories are from fat.

# Cucumber Sandwiches

> 1    *large English cucumber sliced thin*
> 16   *teaspoons Sandwich Spread (page 96)*
> 16   *slices extra-thin wheat bread*

1. Spread 1 teaspoon of spread on each slice of bread.  Place sliced cucumber on one slice and top with another.  Cut off crusts, cut sandwiches, and cover.

Makes 8 sandwiches.  1 serving = 1 sandwich

*Each serving contains:*
> 66   *calories*
> 3    *grams protein*
> 12   *grams carbohydrate*
> 1    *gram fat*
> 128  *mgs. sodium*
> 2    *mgs. cholesterol*
> 3    *grams dietary fiber*

*ADA Exchange Value:*
> $1/2$   *Starch/Bread*
> 1     *Vegetable*
> 14%   *of total calories are from fat.*

# Asparagus and Spinach Soup

1 **pound fresh asparagus**
1 **10-ounce package frozen chopped spinach**
2 **large potatoes diced**
6 **cups low-salt Chicken Broth (page 53)**
1 **teaspoon white pepper**
1 **cup nonfat milk**

1. Cut tips off asparagus and set aside. Cut off bottom ½ inch and discard. Cut remaining stem into small pieces.
2. Bring Chicken Broth to a boil. Add asparagus stems, cover, reduce heat, and simmer ½ hour.
3. Add thawed spinach, diced potatoes, pepper, and nonfat milk. Cover and simmer ½ hour more.
4. Pour soup into food processor with steel blade or blender and puree.
5. Pour soup back into saucepan. Add asparagus tips, cover, and simmer 10 minutes.

Makes 6 servings.

*Each serving contains:*
114 *calories*
6 *grams protein*
22 *grams carbohydrate*
1 *gram fat*
250 *mgs. sodium*
2 *mgs. cholesterol*
3 *grams dietary fiber*

*ADA Exchange Value:*
1 *Starch/Bread*
2 *Vegetable*
8% *of total calories are from fat.*

# Carrot, Leek, and Potato Soup

        5   cups low-salt Chicken Broth (page 53)
        2   leeks, washed and thinly sliced
        2   sticks celery, sliced
        3   large potatoes diced with skin
        2   carrots, grated
       1/2  cup nonfat milk
       1/2  teaspoon ground white pepper

1. Place 1/4 cup of the chicken broth in a Dutch oven and bring to a boil.  Add leeks and celery and "stir fry," tossing vegetables quickly for 2 minutes.
2. Add remaining chicken broth, potatoes, carrots, and pepper and bring to boil.  Reduce heat, cover, and simmer 1/2 hour.
3. Puree mixture either in food processor or blender.  Return soup to Dutch oven and add milk, heat, and serve.

Makes 6 servings.

**Each serving contains:**
       100   calories
         4   grams protein
        21   grams carbohydrate
             negligible grams fat
       200   mgs. sodium
         1   mg. cholesterol
         3   grams dietary fiber

**ADA Exchange Value:**
       1/2   Starch/Bread
         2   Vegetable
             Negligible fat calories.

# Basic White Sauce

The most common of English sauces, the Basic White Sauce is very simple to make and you can add different flavorings to compliment your dish.

> **2  tablespoons flour**
> **1  tablespoon Butter Buds™ , dry**
> **1  cup nonfat milk**

1. Mix all ingredients together thoroughly.  Pour sauce into a saucepan, stirring constantly.  Bring to a boil, reduce heat, and keep stirring until sauce reaches desired thickness.

Items you can add to flavor:
   Celery salt
   Lemon juice (mock hollandaise)
   Worcestershire sauce
   Sherry
   Onion juice
   Chopped parsley
   Chopped chives
   Tarragon
Makes 4 servings.

*Each serving contains:*
> **41  calories**
> **3  grams protein**
> **7  grams carbohydrate**
> **negligible grams fat**
> **81  mgs. sodium**
> **1  mg. cholesterol**
> **Negligible grams dietary fiber**

*ADA Exchange Value:*
> **¹/₂  Nonfat Milk**
> **Negligible fat calories.**

# Mixed Vegetable Salad

- 2 medium beets, cooked crisp but tender and chopped
- 2 medium carrots, cooked crisp but tender and chopped
- 4 red potatoes, cooked tender and chopped
- 1/2 English cucumber, chopped
- 3 pickled gherkins, chopped
- 1 cup frozen baby peas, cooked
- 2 tablespoons low-calorie mayonnaise
- 3 tablespoons low-fat sour cream
- 1/8 teaspoon white pepper

1. Mix all ingredients together, cover, and chill.

Makes 6 servings.

*Each serving contains:*
- 125 calories
- 4 grams protein
- 22 grams carbohydrate
- 3 grams fat
- 148 mgs. sodium
- 3 mgs. cholesterol
- 5 grams dietary fiber

*ADA Exchange Value:*
- 1 Starch/Bread
- 1 Vegetable
- 1/2 Fat
- 22% of total calories are from fat.

# Beetroot Salad

4   fresh beets, grated
2   green apples, grated
2   ounces walnuts, diced
2   cloves garlic, crushed
4   tablespoons low-calorie mayonnaise

1. Mix all ingredients together, cover, and chill for 1 hour.

Makes 6 servings.

*Each serving contains:*
94   *calories*
2   *grams protein*
13   *grams carbohydrate*
4   *grams fat*
94   *mgs. sodium*
1   *mg. cholesterol*
4   *grams dietary fiber*

*ADA Exchange Value:*
$^1/_2$   *Fruit*
1   *Vegetable*
38%   *of total calories are from fat.*

# Crab Salad

4   red potatoes, cooked and cubed
1   red apple, cored and cubed
$1/2$   English cucumber, diced
2   hard-boiled eggs, peeled and chopped
1   cup crab meat (can use imitation)
4   tablespoons low-calorie mayonnaise
4   large red lettuce leaves

1. In a bowl, mix all ingredients except lettuce leaves. Cover and refrigerate 1 hour.
2. Place one lettuce leaf on each of 4 salad plates.
3. Divide the salad mixture into 4 parts and spoon onto the plates. Serve.

Makes 4 servings.

*Each serving contains:*
179   calories
10   grams protein
21   grams carbohydrate
7   grams fat
178   mgs. sodium
75   mgs. cholesterol
3   grams dietary fiber

*ADA Exchange Value:*
1   Lean Meat
1   Starch/Bread
1   Vegetable
1   Fat
35%   of total calories are from fat.

# Creamed Spinach

1   recipe White Sauce (page 104)
2   10-ounce packages frozen chopped spinach,
     thawed, with water squeezed out

1. Make White Sauce.
2. Fold in spinach and heat thoroughly.

Makes 6 servings.

*Each serving contains:*
     53   *calories*
      5   *grams protein*
     10   *grams carbohydrate*
          *negligible grams fat*
    133   *mgs. sodium*
          *negligible mgs. cholesterol*
      3   *grams dietary fiber*

*ADA Exchange Value:*
      2   *Vegetable*
          *Negligible fat calories.*

# Peas in White Sauce

**1  pound package frozen petite peas, thawed**
**1  recipe White Sauce (page 104)**

1. Make White Sauce.
2. Fold in thawed peas and gently simmer until heated.

Makes 6 servings.

*Each serving contains:*

- **90  calories**
- **6  grams protein**
- **16  grams carbohydrate**
  **negligible grams fat**
- **124  mgs. sodium**
  **negligible mgs. cholesterol**
- **6  grams dietary fiber**

*ADA Exchange Value:*

- **1  Starch/Bread**
  **Negligible fat calories.**

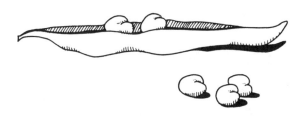

# Onion Potato Cake

*2  pounds potatoes, sliced with skins on*
*1  large onion, thinly sliced*
*6  tablespoons Butter Buds™, liquid*
   *White pepper to taste*

1. Preheat oven to 375 degrees.
2. Spray a 7-inch souffle dish with nonstick spray.
3. In the dish, arrange a layer of potatoes, then a layer of onion. Drizzle with Butter Buds™ and sprinkle with white pepper. Continue layering, finishing with potatoes and 1 tablespoon of the Butter Buds™.
4. Cover and bake for 1¼ hours.
5. Turn out on a round serving platter and serve.

Makes 6 servings.

*Each serving contains:*
- *124  calories*
- *3  grams protein*
- *29  grams carbohydrate*
- *negligible grams fat*
- *58  mgs. sodium*
- *0  mgs. cholesterol*
- *2  grams dietary fiber*

*ADA Exchange Value:*
- *1 ½  Starch/Bread*
- *Negligible fat calories.*

# Baked Stuffed Potatoes

This is a great potato recipe to serve at a dinner party. You can make it ahead and reheat before serving.

> 6   *even-sized russet potatoes*
> 4   *tablespoons Butter Buds™, dry*
> 2/3 *cup nonfat milk, hot*
> 1/2 *teaspoon white pepper*
> 2   *tablespoons chives, chopped*
> 1   *ounce grated Parmesan cheese*

1. Preheat oven to 400 degrees.
2. Scrub the potatoes and prick holes in 4 places with a fork. Bake for 1 hour or until done.
3. Cut top off the potatoes and scoop out the pulp into a bowl.
4. In the bowl with potato pulp, beat in the remaining ingredients. Spoon mixture into the potato shells and reheat before serving.

Makes 6 servings.

*Each serving contains:*
> 132 *calories*
>   4 *grams protein*
>  29 *grams carbohydrate*
>     *negligible grams fat*
> 103 *mgs. sodium*
>   1 *mg. cholesterol*
>   2 *grams dietary fiber*

*ADA Exchange Value:*
> 1 1/2 *Starch/Bread*
>       *Negligible fat calories.*

# Roasted Potatoes

$^1/_2$  *cup low-salt Chicken Broth (page 53)*
  3  *medium russet potatoes, washed and cut into*
     *fourths*
     *Paprika*

1. Preheat oven to 400 degrees.  Spray a cookie sheet with a nonstick spray.
2. In a saucepan, bring Chicken Broth to boil and continue boiling until broth is reduced to $^1/_4$ cup.
3. Place potatoes on cookie sheet.  Brush each chunk with Chicken Broth and sprinkle each with paprika.
4. Roast for 30 minutes or until potatoes are tender.

Makes 6 servings.

*Each serving contains:*
  57  *calories*
   1  *gram protein*
  13  *grams carbohydrate*
      *negligible grams fat*
  50  *mgs. sodium*
   0  *mgs. cholesterol*
   1  *gram dietary fiber*

*ADA Exchange Value:*
  $^3/_4$  *Starch/Bread*
      *Negligible fat calories.*

# Rice with Onions

This is an easy, fool-proof rice dish that holds well in a low oven until time to serve.

> 1   *tablespoon margarine*
> 1   *medium onion, chopped*
> 1   *cup long grain white rice*
> 2 1/4   *cups hot water*

1. Preheat oven to 300 degrees.
2. Melt margarine in an oven-proof saucepan. Saute onion in margarine. Add rice and toss in margarine and onions. Add water and bring to a boil.
3. Cover and place in oven for 30 minutes.

Makes 6 servings.

*Each serving contains:*
> 97   *calories*
> 2   *grams protein*
> 18   *grams carbohydrate*
> 2   *grams fat*
> 15   *mgs. sodium*
> 0   *mgs. cholesterol*
>     *negligible grams dietary fiber*

*ADA Exchange Value:*
> 1   *Starch/Bread*
> 19%   *of total calories are from fat.*

# Salmon Dill Pie

2 cups soft bread crumbs
$^1/_2$ cup nonfat milk
2 egg whites, slightly beaten
$^1/_4$ small onion, finely chopped
2 tablespoons fresh parsley, chopped
1 tablespoon Butter Buds™, liquid
$^1/_2$ teaspoon white pepper
1 pound canned salmon, drained and flaked
4 medium potatoes, cubed with skin on
2 egg whites, slightly beaten
1 recipe White Sauce (page 104)
$^3/_4$ teaspoon dried dill weed
$^1/_2$ cup low-fat sour cream

1. Preheat oven to 350 degrees.
2. Combine bread crumbs, milk, 2 egg whites, onion, parsley, Butter Buds™, and white pepper.
3. Mix in salmon until well blended.
4. Spoon mixture into an 8-inch round dish that has been sprayed with a nonstick spray.
5. In a saucepan, boil the potatoes until done. Drain potatoes and mash them, adding 2 egg whites into potatoes.
6. Pipe or spoon potatoes around salmon mixture.
7. Bake pie for 30 minutes.
8. Make the White Sauce, then add dill weed and sour cream to White Sauce.
9. To serve, cut pie in 6 wedges and put on serving plates. Pour sauce over each wedge.

Makes 6 servings.

*Each serving contains:*
- *270 calories*
- *21 grams protein*
- *46 grams carbohydrate*
- *5 grams fat*
- *355 mgs. sodium*
- *38 mgs. cholesterol*
- *2 grams dietary fiber*

*ADA Exchange Value:*
- *2 Lean Meat*
- *3 Starch/Bread*
- *17% of total calories are from fat.*

# Creamed Chicken

 1   recipe White Sauce (page 104)
 1   leek, thinly sliced (cut off dark green top and
     discard)
 1 ¹/₂  pounds cooked chicken breast, boned and
     skinned
 2 ¹/₂  cups cooked brown rice

1. Make White Sauce in a large saucepan.
2. In a skillet sprayed with a nonstick spray, saute leek until
   tender.
3. Stir leek into White Sauce.
4. Fold in chicken.  Heat thoroughly.
5. Serve over brown rice.

Makes 6 servings.

*Each serving contains:*
- 221   *calories*
- 28   *grams protein*
- 17   *grams carbohydrate*
- 4   *grams fat*
- 109   *mgs. sodium*
- 67   *mgs. cholesterol*
- 1   *gram dietary fiber*

*ADA Exchange Value:*
- 3   *Lean Meat*
- 1   *Starch/Bread*
- 16%   *of total calories are from fat.*

# Beef and Beer

2 1/2   *pounds lean beef, cubed*
  1/2   *teaspoon black pepper*
  2   *large onions, thinly sliced*
  2   *tablespoons flour*
  1   *bottle light beer*
  1/2   *cup low-salt beef broth*

1. Preheat oven to 275 degrees.
2. Toss beef cubes and pepper together.
3. Spray a large skillet with nonstick spray and brown beef cubes. Transfer meat to an oven-proof casserole.
4. Put onions into hot skillet and cook until tender. Sprinkle onions with flour and mix well. Add onions to casserole.
5. Pour beer and broth over meat. Cover casserole and bake 2 hours.

Makes 8 servings.

*Each serving contains:*
  201   *calories*
  26   *grams protein*
  3   *grams carbohydrate*
  8   *grams fat*
  135   *mgs. sodium*
  72   *mgs. cholesterol*
  *negligible grams dietary fiber*

*ADA Exchange Value:*
  3   *Lean Meat*
  1   *Vegetable*
  36%   *of total calories are from fat.*

# Macaroni and Cheese

> 1 **pound penne (or your favorite macaroni)**
> 4 **cups nonfat milk**
> 1 **tablespoon Butter Buds™, dry**
> 6 **tablespoons flour**
> 1/2 **teaspoon white pepper**
> 1/4 **teaspoon cayenne pepper**
> 4 **ounces sharp cheddar cheese, grated**

1. Cook macaroni in a large pot of boiling water until just tender. Pour into colander and rinse with cold water. Drain well and set aside.
2. Preheat oven to 350 degrees.
3. In a large saucepan, mix milk, Butter Buds™, flour, and peppers together and bring to boil, stirring constantly. Reduce heat. When mixture thickens, add grated cheese and continue stirring until melted.
4. Mix the cheese sauce and macaroni together in an oven-proof casserole. Cover and bake 20 minutes. Uncover and bake another 5 minutes.

Makes 6 servings.

*Each serving contains:*
> 278 *calories*
> 13 *grams protein*
> 43 *grams carbohydrate*
> 6 *grams fat*
> 177 *mgs. sodium*
> 17 *mgs. cholesterol*
> 1 *gram dietary fiber*

*ADA Exchange Value:*
> 2 *Medium-Fat Meat*
> 3 *Starch/Bread*
> 19% *of total calories are from fat.*

# Sponge Cake

This is a basic cake that you can fill with sugar-free jam, custard, yogurt cream, or chocolate mousse.

> 1 1/2  *cups self-rising flour*
> *Grated peel from 1/2 lemon*
> 3/4  *cup nonfat plain yogurt*
> 1  *cup nonfat milk*
> 1/4  *cup fructose*
> 4  *egg whites, room temperature*

1. Preheat oven to 350 degrees.  Grease 2 8-inch round cake pans.
2. Sift flour into a bowl.  Stir in lemon rind.
3. Mix yogurt, milk, and fructose together.
4. Whip egg whites to soft peaks.
5. Fold yogurt mixture into egg whites.
6. Fold flour into mixture.
7. Divide into pans and bake 25 minutes or until cake springs back when touched.
8. Cool on racks.

Makes 8 servings.

*Each serving contains:*
> 120  *calories*
> 6  *grams protein*
> 22  *grams carbohydrate*
> 0  *grams fat*
> 100  *mgs. sodium*
> 0  *mgs. cholesterol*
> 1  *gram dietary fiber*

*ADA Exchange Value:*
> 1  *Starch/Bread*
> 1/2  *Fruit*
> 1/2  *Lean Meat*
> *negligible fat calories.*

# Orange Tea Loaf

       2   cups self-rising flour
  1 ¹/₂   teaspoons baking powder
      ³/₄   cup nonfat plain yogurt
      ¹/₂   cup fructose
       2   egg whites, room temperature
            Grated peel of 1/2 orange
       2   tablespoons orange juice
      ¹/₂   cup nonfat milk

1. Preheat oven to 375 degrees.  Spray an 8- by 4-inch loaf pan with nonstick spray.
2. Sift flour and baking powder together in a bowl.  Set aside.
3. Mix yogurt and fructose together.  Set aside.
4. Beat egg whites to soft peaks.
5. Fold orange juice, orange peel, yogurt mixture, and milk into egg whites.
6. Fold flour into egg white mixture.
7. Pour batter into loaf pan and bake 40 to 50 minutes or until a toothpick comes out clean.
8. Cool 10 minutes, then turn out on wire rack and cool 15 minutes.  Wrap with plastic wrap and refrigerate 24 hours.

Makes 8 servings.

*Each serving contains:*
       *166   calories*
          *5   grams protein*
        *34   grams carbohydrate*
          *0   grams fat*
      *125   mgs. sodium*
          *0   mgs. cholesterol*
          *1   gram dietary fiber*

*ADA Exchange Value:*
          *1   Starch/Bread*
          *1   Fruit*
               *Negligible fat calories.*

# Quick Scones

1 1/3   **cups Wheaties**™
  2/3   **cup self-rising flour**
  1/4   **cup raisins**
   1   **tablespoon fructose**
   1   **tablespoon molasses**
  3/4   **cup nonfat milk**
   2   **tablespoons Butter Buds**™ **, dry**

1. Preheat oven to 400 degrees. Spray a cookie sheet with nonstick spray.
2. Combine Wheaties™ and flour. Mix in raisins, fructose, molasses, milk, and Butter Buds™.
3. Drop by tablespoonfuls onto cookie sheet, 2 inches apart. Bake 10 to 12 minutes or until golden brown.

Makes 6 servings.

**Each serving contains:**
   117   **calories**
     3   **grams protein**
    26   **grams carbohydrate**
       **negligible grams fat**
   157   **mgs. sodium**
       **negligible mgs. cholesterol**
     1   **gram dietary fiber**

**ADA Exchange Value:**
1 1/2   **Starch/Bread**
       **Negligible fat calories.**

# Crumpet Scones

These are very easy and come out like thick pancakes.

> 1   *cup all-purpose flour*
> ¹/₄   *teaspoon baking soda*
> 2   *tablespoons fructose*
> ²/₃   *cup low-fat buttermilk*
> 2   *egg whites, slightly beaten*
> 2   *teaspoons Butter Buds™, liquid*

1. Sift flour and baking soda together.
2. Mix in the remaining ingredients.
3. On a preheated griddle or large heavy skillet sprayed with a nonstick spray, pour a large spoonful of batter.  When it is full of bubbles, flip over using spatula.
3. Put scones in a basket lined with cloth or paper towels.  Serve immediately.  Scones can be reheated in your toaster if you have any leftover.

Makes 8 servings.

*Each serving contains:*
> 75   *calories*
> 3   *grams protein*
> 15   *grams carbohydrate*
>    *negligible grams fat*
> 81   *mgs. sodium*
>    *negligible mgs. cholesterol*
>    *negligible grams dietary fiber*

*ADA Exchange Value:*
> 1   *Starch/Bread*
>    *negligible fat calories.*

# Fruit Scones

These are heavier scones with a bit more flavor than plain oven scones, and can be served with jam, yogurt cream, or alone.

**2 1/2  cups all-purpose flour**
**2  teaspoons baking powder**
**1  teaspoon baking soda**
**1/3  cup fructose**
**3  tablespoons Butter Buds™, dry**
**1/2  cup raisins**
**2  egg whites, slightly beaten**
**1 1/2  cups nonfat plain yogurt**
**Grated peel of 1 lemon**
**Nonfat milk for brushing scones**

1. Preheat oven to 425 degrees. Spray a large cookie sheet with nonstick spray.
2. Sift flour, baking powder, and baking soda together.
3. With a fork, stir in sugar, Butter Buds™, raisins, egg whites, yogurt, and lemon peel until dough barely holds together.
4. Turn onto a floured surface and roll out with a floured rolling pin or pat out to 1/2 inch thick. With a cookie cutter (it's fun to use different shapes) cut out and place 1 inch apart on cookie sheet. Brush tops with nonfat milk.
5. Bake 10 to 12 minutes or until they are golden and well risen.

Makes 8 servings.

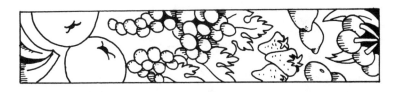

*Each serving contains:*
- *115   calories*
- *4   grams protein*
- *24   grams carbohydrate*
- *1   gram fat*
- *184   mgs. sodium*
- *negligible mgs. cholesterol*
- *1   gram dietary fiber*

*ADA Exchange Value:*
- *1   Starch/Bread*
- *1/2   Fruit*
- *7%   of total calories are from fat.*

# Sherry Trifle

The trifle is one of the most often-served English desserts. It is popular at high tea and at Christmas.

- 1 **Sponge Cake (page 119)**
- 1/2 **cup sugar-free raspberry jam**
- 1/2 **cup sweet sherry**
- 4 **peaches, thinly sliced**
- 4 **tablespoons corn starch**
- 2 **cups 1% milk**
- 1 **teaspoon vanilla**
- 5 **packages Equal™**
- 1/2 **cup toasted almonds, chopped**
- 2 **cups low-calorie whipped topping (optional)**
- 1 **cup raspberries**

1. Spread cake with jam, cut in pieces, and place in a large, pretty bowl.
2. Pour sherry over cake and cover all with the peaches.
3. In a saucepan, mix milk and cornstarch. Bring to boil, stirring constantly. Add vanilla and stir until thickened (like pudding). Remove from heat, stir in Equal™, and let cool.
4. Pour cooled pudding over cake in bowl. Sprinkle top with almonds.
5. Spread on whipped topping, then put berries over top. If you are not using the whipped topping, put the berries over the pudding.

Makes 12 servings.

*Each serving contains:*
- 227 *calories*
- 7 *grams protein*
- 39 *grams carbohydrate*
- 4 *grams fat*
- 113 *mgs. sodium*
- 2 *mgs. cholesterol*
- 2 *grams dietary fiber*

*ADA Exchange Value:*
- 2 *Starch/Bread*
- 1/2 *Fruit*
- 1 *Fat*
- 16% *of total calories are from fat.*

# Chocolate-Filled Sponge Cake

   3  *tablespoons cornstarch*
   3  *tablespoons imported cocoa powder,*
      *unsweetened*
   1  *cup nonfat milk*
   1  *teaspoon vanilla*
   3  *packages of Equal*™
   3  *tablespoons sugar-free raspberry jelly*
   1  *Sponge Cake (page 119)*

1. Mix cornstarch and cocoa together in a saucepan. Slowly add milk, stirring constantly.
2. Bring to a boil. Add vanilla and continue stirring until thick. Turn off heat and add Equal™. Let cool slightly.
3. Spread the raspberry jelly on the sponge cake, then spread one half of chocolate mixture on cake. Top with the other cake half and spread the remaining mixture over the top.

Makes 8 servings.

*Each serving contains:*
   161  *calories*
     8  *grams protein*
    35  *grams carbohydrate*
     3  *grams fat*
    80  *mgs. sodium*
     1  *mg. cholesterol*
     2  *grams dietary fiber*

*ADA Exchange Value:*
    2  *Starch/Bread*
  17%  *of total calories are from fat.*

# Scandinavian
# Cuisine

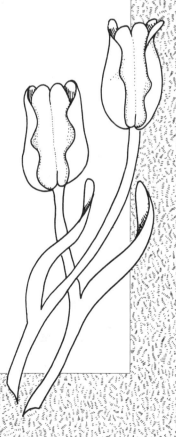

# Scandinavia

Our fair-haired and fair-skinned friends in northern Europe are known for their fresh and preserved or pickled foods. Each Scandinavian country has its own specialties. Dairy products, especially cheese, are popular. Pickled vegetables and pickled fishes, especially herring, are often used as a base for hot and cold dishes. Bread and potatoes are ever popular in Europe. Fresh breads as well as a variety of unleavened breads are used as a base for open-face sandwiches.

Perhaps one of the more common associations we make with Scandinavian cuisine is the smorgasbord—a display of cold foods that would rival any salad bar and a centuries-old precursor to grazing. Try a smorgasbord for your next gathering. It's a great idea for an outdoor affair or even a picnic.

### Smorgasbord

Cold Poached Salmon
with Mustard Dill Sauce

Fish Salad

Pickled Fish

Pickled Beet Salad

Cucumbers in Sour Cream

Mushroom Salad

Bakery Breads:
Swedish Rye
Caraway Rye

Unleavened flat bread crackers such as Rye Krisp™ or Kavli™

Platter of crisp lettuce leaves and tomato wedges

Platter of fresh fruit

# Swedish Pancakes

1   *whole egg*
4   *egg whites*
1   *cup nonfat milk*
1   *cup flour*
1   *tablespoon fructose*

1. In a medium-size bowl combine whole egg and egg whites and stir to mix well.  Stir in milk.
2. Stir flour and fructose into milk and egg mixture, beating by hand until well mixed.  Batter will be thin like crepe batter.
3. Spray a griddle or skillet with nonstick spray and heat to the point at which a drop of water sizzles in the pan.  For each pancake, carefully pour 2 tablespoons of batter into pan, making 3 or 4 pancakes at a time.  When brown on the edges and bubbly in the center, turn and cook briefly on the other side.  Remove to a heated platter to keep warm.
4. Serve with fresh fruit or sugar-free preserves.

Makes 6 servings.

**Each serving contains:**
- 117  *calories*
- 7  *grams protein*
- 18  *grams carbohydrate*
- 2  *grams fat*
- 68  *mgs. sodium*
- 47  *mgs. cholesterol*
- *negligible grams dietary fiber*

**ADA Exchange Value:**
- 1  *Starch/Bread*
- $1/2$  *Medium-fat Meat*
- 15%  *of total calories are from fat.*

# Sour Cream Waffles

2   *eggs*
4   *egg whites*
1   *tablespoon fructose*
1   *cup flour*
1   *teaspoon cardamon*
$^1/_2$   *teaspoon cinnamon*
1   *cup reduced-calorie sour cream*
1   *tablespoon oil*

1. Mix eggs and egg whites until combined.  Add fructose.
2. Add cinnamon and cardamon to flour, then stir flour into egg mixture.  Add sour cream and oil and stir just to mix.
3. Spray a waffle iron with nonstick spray and heat.  Pour $^1/_2$ cup of waffle batter into preheated iron and bake until nicely browned.  Continue until all batter is used.

Makes 6 servings.  1 serving = 1 waffle

*Each serving contains:*

  159   *calories*
    8   *grams protein*
   18   *grams carbohydrate*
    6   *grams fat*
   80   *mgs. sodium*
   50   *mgs. cholesterol*
        *negligible grams dietary fiber*

*ADA Exchange Value:*
    1   *Starch/Bread*
  $^1/_2$   *Lean Meat*
    1   *Fat*
  34%   *of total calories are from fat.*

# Potato Leek Soup

2   tablespoons Butter Buds™, liquid
3   leeks, white part only
3   medium potatoes
2   stalks celery, chopped
3   cups low-salt Chicken Broth (page 53)
2   cups 1% milk
    Parsley

1. Wash leeks well and slice thinly. Pour Butter Buds™ into a large soup pot. Heat and add sliced leeks and celery. Cook and stir for several minutes, taking care not to burn.
2. Peel potatoes (if desired). Cut into quarters lengthwise, then dice into medium-size chunks. Add to soup pot.
3. Pour in Chicken Broth and simmer soup for 20 to 30 minutes or until potatoes seem tender. Slowly pour in milk and heat but do not boil.
4. Serve soup as is or process soup in a food processor to give it a smooth, cream-like consistency. Garnish with parsley.

Makes 8 servings.  1 serving = 1 cup

*Each serving contains:*
        83   *calories*
         4   *grams protein*
        16   *grams carbohydrate*
         1   *gram fat*
       100   *mgs. sodium*
         3   *mgs. cholesterol*
         2   *grams dietary fiber*

*ADA Exchange Value:*
         1   *Starch/Bread*
       11%   *of total calories are from fat.*

# Fresh Spinach Soup

*8 cups Chicken Broth (page 53)*
*2 bunches fresh spinach, washed, with large stems removed*
*2 tablespoons Butter Buds™, dry*
*1/8 teaspoon nutmeg*

1. Bring Chicken Broth to a boil in a large soup kettle.
2. Chop spinach coarsely and place in pot with broth. Simmer uncovered 6 to 8 minutes, then pour the broth and spinach into a sieve set over a large bowl. Press down on the spinach remaining in sieve to remove as much moisture as possible.
3. Set aside ¼ cup broth and let cool. Return remaining broth to the pot and bring to a boil. Combine the flour and dry Butter Buds™ with ¼ cup room-temperature broth. Mix until very smooth. Pour slowly into hot broth, stirring constantly with a whisk. Allow mixture to simmer for a few minutes.
4. Chop cooked spinach until fine and return to soup pot. Add nutmeg, heat, and serve.

Makes 8 servings. 1 serving = 1 cup

*Each serving contains:*
- *33 calories*
- *3 grams protein*
- *4 grams carbohydrate*
- *0 grams fat*
- *60 mgs. sodium*
- *0 mgs. cholesterol*
- *2 grams dietary fiber*

*ADA Exchange Value:*
*1 ½ Vegetable*
*negligible fat calories.*

# Fresh Green Bean Salad

3 tablespoons red wine vinegar
1 tablespoon olive oil
$^1/_2$ cup Chicken Broth (page 53)
  Fresh ground black pepper
1 tablespoon fresh dill, finely chopped
1 tablespoon fresh parsley, finely chopped
1 sprig savory ($^1/_2$ teaspoon dried summer savory)
1 pound fresh green beans

1. In a small bowl combine vinegar, oil, chicken stock, and a few grindings of pepper. Beat well with a whisk to blend thoroughly. Stir in dill, parsley, and savory. Cover bowl and set aside.
2. Trim ends off beans, then steam for 3 to 5 minutes over boiling water until beans are crisp but tender. Remove from heat at once and plunge into very cold water or ice water. As beans cool, drain them well or pat dry.
3. Transfer beans to a large mixing bowl and pour dressing over them, stirring to coat. Chill for at least 1 hour before serving.

Makes 6 servings.

*Each serving contains:*
  45 calories
   2 grams protein
   5 grams carbohydrate
   3 grams fat
  40 mgs. sodium
   0 mgs. cholesterol
   2 grams dietary fiber

*ADA Exchange Value:*
   1 Vegetable
  $^1/_2$ Fat
  60% of total calories are from fat.

# Pickled Beet Salad

Delicious and flavorful.

   8  *fresh beets (see note below)*
   1/2  *cup red wine vinegar*
   1/2  *cup cider vinegar*
   1  *onion, peeled and thinly sliced*
   4  *whole cloves*
   1/2  *teaspoon ground coriander seeds*
   6  *whole black peppercorns*
   1  *tablespoon horseradish (optional)*

1. Scrub beets and cut off ends. Steam over boiling water until just done. Remove from steamer and plunge into cold water. Remove skins and drain.
2. Slice beets into 1/8-inch slices and place them into a deep ceramic or glass bowl.
3. In a medium-size steel or enamel saucepan, bring the vinegars, onion, cloves, coriander, and peppercorns to a boil over high heat. Pour the mixture over beets. Be sure the beets are fully covered by the marinade. If not, add a little more vinegar. Cover and refrigerate 24 hours to marinate.
4. Just before serving remove the cloves and peppercorns. Mix the horseradish with 2 tablespoons of beet juice, then pour over beets and stir gently to mix. Serve on a lettuce leaf or as a garnish.

NOTE: Use fresh beets with tops. Remove the tops before preparing beets. Wash and steam tops for a few minutes. Beet greens or beet tops are a delicious and different green vegetable. Serve with a little vinegar and Butter Buds™ mixed in.

Makes 6 servings.

*Each serving contains:*
- 22 *calories*
- 1 *gram protein*
- 6 *grams carbohydrate*
- 0 *fat*
- 26 *mgs. sodium*
- 0 *cholesterol*
- 1 *gram dietary fiber*

*ADA Exchange Value:*
- 1 *Vegetable*
  *Negligible fat calories.*

# Scandinavian Cabbage

A quick and easy recipe that serves generous portions.

> 1   **small head cabbage, coarsely shredded**
> 1   **cup reduced-calorie sour cream**
> 1   **teaspoon caraway seed**
> 1/4  **teaspoon freshly ground pepper**

1. Steam cabbage until crisp but tender.  Remove to another pan.
2. Stir rest of ingredients into cabbage and heat carefully just to heat through.  Serve.

Makes 6 servings.

*Each serving contains:*

> 56   *calories*
>  2   *grams protein*
>  4   *grams carbohydrate*
>  4   *grams fat*
> 27   *mgs. sodium*
>  8   *mgs. cholesterol*
>  1   *gram dietary fiber*

*ADA Exchange Value:*

> 1   *Vegetable*
> 1   *Fat*
> 64%  *of total calories are from fat.*

# Pickled Fish

A delicious substitute for salted fishes, such as pickled herring.
Use as an appetizer on a toothpick.

> 1   *pound firm white fish, about $1/2$ -inch thick*
> 1   *onion, sliced into rings*
> 1   *carrot, sliced*
> $2/3$   *cup white vinegar*
> $1/4$   *cup water*
> 3   *bay leaves*

1. Bring a pot of water to a boil. Rinse fish well, then pat dry.
   Cut into cubes about 1- by 1-inch. Drop a few cubes of fish
   one at a time into boiling water. Remove pieces with a slotted
   spoon after about 10 seconds in the water. Continue until all
   fish has been blanched. Drain fish pieces and place them into
   a shallow glass or ceramic dish.
2. Spray another pan with nonstick spray and lightly saute onions
   and carrots until onions just begin to turn opaque. Do not
   brown. Add the vinegar, water, and bay leaf and bring to a
   boil. Reduce heat and simmer about 5 minutes.
3. Pour the hot vinegar mixture over the fish cubes, allowing
   onions and carrots to lay decoratively on top. Cover and place
   in refrigerator for 24 hours. Use as part of the Smorgasbord
   or for any recipes needing pickled fish.

Makes 8 servings.

*Each serving contains:*
> 71   *calories*
> 13   *grams protein*
> 3   *grams carbohydrate*
> 1   *gram fat*
> 48   *mgs. sodium*
> 32   *mgs. cholesterol*
> 1   *gram dietary fiber*

*ADA Exchange Value:*
> 2   *Lean Meat*
> 13%   *of total calories are from fat.*

# Cucumbers in Sour Cream

    2   cups cucumber, thinly sliced (about 2 medium
        cucumbers)
  1/4   cup reduced-calorie sour cream
    2   tablespoons Dijon-style mustard
    2   tablespoons white vinegar
1/2 to 1   teaspoon fructose
        Freshly ground pepper
  1/2   teaspoon dried dill weed or 1 teaspoon fresh
        minced dill weed

1. Place sliced cucumbers into a bowl.
2. In another bowl combine rest of ingredients and mix well.
   Pour over cucumbers and stir to mix.  Chill and serve.

Makes 4 servings.

*Each serving contains:*
   28   calories
    1   gram protein
    4   grams carbohydrate
    1   gram fat
   14   mgs. sodium
    3   mgs. cholesterol
    1   gram dietary fiber

*ADA Exchange Value:*
    1   Vegetable
   32%   of total calories are from fat.

# Sour Cream Potato Salad

4   medium potatoes, cooked and diced
1/2  cup cucumber, diced
1   tablespoon onion, minced
3/4  teaspoon celery seed
1/4  teaspoon pepper
2   hard-cooked eggs, whites only
1/4  cup reduced-calorie sour cream
1/4  cup nonfat yogurt
2   tablespoons vinegar
1/2  teaspoon dry mustard

1. Combine potatoes, cucumber, onion, celery seed, pepper, and egg whites in a mixing bowl.
2. In another small bowl combine sour cream and yogurt. Stir in vinegar and dry mustard and mix very well. Pour over potato mixture and stir just enough to mix or coat potatoes. Serve.

Makes 6 servings. 1 serving = 1/2 cup

*Each serving contains:*

82  *calories*
3  *grams protein*
16  *grams carbohydrate*
1  *gram fat*
33  *mgs. sodium*
2  *mgs. cholesterol*
2  *grams dietary fiber*

*ADA Exchange Value:*

1  *Starch/Bread*
11%  *of total calories are from fat.*

# Fish Salad

| | |
|---|---|
| 1/2 | recipe Pickled Fish (page 139) |
| 4 | small red potatoes, cooked with skins on, then diced |
| 2 | tablespoons onion, finely chopped |
| 1 | tablespoon horseradish sauce |
| 1 | teaspoon juice from Pickled Fish |
| 3 | tablespoons reduced-calorie sour cream |
| 3 | tablespoons nonfat yogurt |
| 2 | tablespoons fresh dill, chopped |
| | Freshly ground pepper |
| 2 | hard-boiled eggs, whites only, sliced into strips |
| 2 | fresh tomatoes, cut into wedges |
| 6 | lettuce leaves |

1. With your hands, lightly crumble pickled fish into small chunks.
2. Place potatoes and fish into a serving bowl.
3. In another bowl combine horseradish, pickling juice, sour cream, yogurt, dill, and a few grinds of pepper. Stir to mix well.
4. Pour dressing over fish and potatoes. Cover and keep in refrigerator at least 30 minutes before serving.
5. To serve, place 6 lettuce leaves on separate plates and spoon some fish salad on top of each leaf. Garnish with sliced egg whites and tomato wedges.

Makes 6 servings.

*Each serving contains:*

| | | | |
|---|---|---|---|
| 127 | calories | | |
| 13 | grams protein | | |
| 15 | grams carbohydrate | **ADA Exchange Value:** | |
| 2 | grams fat | 1 | Lean Meat |
| 72 | mgs. sodium | 1/2 | Starch/Bread |
| 116 | mgs. cholesterol | 1 | Vegetable |
| 2 | grams dietary fiber | 14% | of total calories are from fat. |

# Mushroom Salad

*1/2* *pound fresh mushrooms, cleaned and sliced*
*1* *cup water*
*Juice of 1/2 lemon*

*Dressing:*
*3* *tablespoons reduced-calorie sour cream*
*1* *tablespoon nonfat yogurt*
*1* *tablespoon onion, finely minced*
*1* *tablespoon white wine*

1. In a small pot bring water and lemon juice to a boil. Add sliced mushrooms, reduce heat, cover, and cook about 3 minutes. Drain mushrooms, then pat dry with paper towels. Place in a serving dish.
2. Combine dressing ingredients in a small dish and mix well. Gently stir dressing into mushrooms. Serve as a garnish or salad.

Makes 4 servings.

*Each serving contains:*
*47* *calories*
*4* *grams protein*
*6* *grams carbohydrate*
*1* *gram fat*
*47* *mgs. sodium*
*2* *mgs. cholesterol*
*1* *gram dietary fiber*

*ADA Exchange Value:*
*1 1/2* *Vegetable*
*19%* *of total calories are from fat.*

# Rice Casserole

A delicious way to use leftover brown or white rice.

   2   *cups cooked rice*
 *¹/₄*  *pound mushrooms, sliced*
   1   *small onion, chopped*
   2   *medium tomatoes, chopped*
   2   *teaspoons marjoram (may use any herb for seasoning)*
       *Freshly ground pepper*
   1   *ounce goat cheese (or any reduced-calorie cheese)*
       *Parsley*

1. Preheat oven to 350 degrees.
2. Place rice in a casserole dish.
3. Spray a frying pan with nonstick spray. Saute mushrooms and onions until tender. Stir in tomatoes, marjoram, and pepper. Stir and cook just enough to heat through.
4. Pour vegetable mixture over rice and stir to mix. Crumble or grate cheese over top. Cover and heat for 20 to 30 minutes, just until heated through. Garnish with parsley.

Makes 6 servings. 1 serving = ¹/₂ cup

*Each serving contains:*
 *100  calories*
   *3  grams protein*
  *20  grams carbohydrate*
   *1  gram fat*
  *28  mgs. sodium*
   *3  mgs. cholesterol*
   *1  gram dietary fiber*

*ADA Exchange Value:*
   *1  Starch/Bread*
   *1  Vegetable*
  *9%  of total calories are from fat.*

EUROPEAN CUISINE FROM THE GUILTLESS GOURMET

# Swedish Meatballs

- 1 pound lean ground meat (Use beef, pork, veal, or a combination)
- 1/2 onion, finely chopped
- 1 large potato, boiled and mashed (about 1 cup)
- 3 tablespoons fine dry bread crumbs
- 2 tablespoons reduced-calorie sour cream
- 2 tablespoons nonfat yogurt
- 2 egg whites
- 1 tablespoon parsley, finely chopped

1. Combine all ingredients and mix thoroughly. Shape into 32 small meatballs. Place onto a flat tray, cover, and refrigerate at least 1 hour before cooking.
2. When ready to cook, spray a heavy skillet with nonstick spray and heat to a moderate temperature. Add about half the meatballs and cook until well browned on all sides and cooked through. Repeat this process with the rest of the meatballs until all are cooked.

Makes 8 servings. 1 serving = 4 meatballs

*Each serving contains:*
- 108 calories
- 15 grams protein
- 6 grams carbohydrate
- 2 grams fat
- 60 mgs. sodium
- 38 mgs. cholesterol
- 1 gram dietary fiber

*ADA Exchange Value:*
- 2 Lean Meat
- 1 Vegetable
- 17% of total calories are from fat.

# Baked Fish with Fresh Tomato Sauce

  1  *pound fresh or frozen fish steaks or filets*
  4  *tomatoes*
  1/2  *onion, chopped*
  1  *tablespoon capers*
  1  *bay leaf*
  2  *tablespoons Butter Buds™, liquid*
     *Freshly ground black pepper*

1. Preheat oven to 350 degrees.
2. Rinse fish, pat dry, and place in a baking dish.  Season with Butter Buds™ and pepper.  Bake until done.  (Length of baking time will depend on thickness of fish.)  Remove fish from oven.
3. Meanwhile, fill a saucepan with water and bring to a boil.  Dip tomatoes into boiling water, then immediately plunge into cold water in order to remove skins.  Cut tomatoes in half and remove seeds.  Dice tomato flesh and set aside.
4. Spray a small skillet with nonstick spray.  Saute onions until soft and just beginning to brown.  Stir in tomatoes, capers, and bay leaf.  Cover and simmer about 15 minutes.  When fish is done baking, place each serving on a plate and top with about 1/4 cup of tomato sauce.

Makes 4 servings.

*Each serving contains:*

  154  *calories*
   27  *grams protein*
    8  *grams carbohydrate*
    1  *gram fat*
  225  *mgs. sodium*
   64  *mgs. cholesterol*
    2  *grams dietary fiber*

*ADA Exchange Value:*

  3  *Lean Meat*
  1  *Vegetable*
  6%  *of total calories are from fat.*

EUROPEAN CUISINE FROM THE GUILTLESS GOURMET

# Poached Salmon with Mustard Dill Sauce

> 1 pound fresh salmon steaks or filets

**Poaching Liquid:**
> 1 1/2 cups water
> 1/2 cup white wine
> 1 stalk celery, chopped
> 1/4 cup parsley, chopped

**Sauce:**
> 2 tablespoons Dijon-style mustard
> 1 tablespoon white wine
> 1/4 cup reduced-calorie sour cream
> 1 tablespoon fresh dill, chopped

1. Combine water, wine, celery, and parsley in a pan and bring to a boil. Reduce to simmer and place rinsed salmon into poaching liquid. Cover and poach until done, about 10 minutes, depending on thickness of fish.
2. Combine the sauce ingredients in a small bowl and mix well. When fish is done, carefully remove it to a platter or serving dish with a slotted spoon or spatula. Serve sauce as a garnish or on the side.

Makes 4 servings.

**Each serving contains:**
> 204 calories
> 32 grams protein
> 3 grams carbohydrate
> 7 grams fat
> 200 mgs. sodium
> 35 mgs. cholesterol
> 1 gram dietary fiber

**ADA Exchange Value:**
> 4 Lean Meat
> 31% of total calories are from fat.

# Baked Fish with Cucumber Sauce

*1 pound fresh white fish fillets or steaks*
*¼ cup cucumber, peeled and finely chopped*
*2 tablespoons reduced-calorie sour cream*
*2 tablespoons nonfat yogurt*
*1 tablespoon onion, freshly minced*
*1 tablespoon fresh dill, chopped*

1. Preheat oven to 350 degrees.
2. Rinse fish and pat dry.  Place fish in a baking dish and bake until done.  Time will vary according to thickness of fish.
3. Combine rest of ingredients in a small bowl and mix thoroughly.  When fish is done baking, divide onto 4 plates and garnish each with about 2 tablespoons of sauce.

Makes 4 servings.

*Each serving contains:*
- *122 calories*
- *27 grams protein*
- *2 grams carbohydrate*
- *1 gram fat*
- *99 mgs. sodium*
- *55 mgs. cholesterol*
- *negligible grams dietary fiber*

*ADA Exchange Value:*
- *3 Lean Meat*
- *7% of total calories are from fat.*

# Chocolate Sauce

A good, very low-calorie sauce that has a rich taste. We recommend using an imported cocoa powder for the best result.

> $^1/_2$   *cup water*
> $^1/_4$   *cup fructose*
> $^1/_4$   *cup imported dry cocoa powder*

1. Combine water and fructose in a small saucepan and bring to a boil. Boil for about 2 minutes, then remove from heat.
2. Stir in cocoa powder all at once and beat with a wire whisk until smooth and glossy. It will thicken slightly.

Makes $^3/_4$ cup. 1 serving = 1 tablespoon

*Each serving contains:*
>   22   *calories*
>         *negligible grams protein*
>    4   *grams carbohydrate*
>    1   *gram fat*
>    5   *mgs. sodium*
>    0   *mgs. cholesterol*
>         *negligible grams dietary fiber*

*ADA Exchange Value:*
>  $^1/_4$   *Fruit*
>  *41%   of total calories are from fat.*

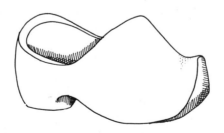

# Baked Meringues

**4 egg whites, at room temperature**
**¹/₈ teaspoon cream of tartar**
**8 packages Equal ™**

1. Preheat oven to 250 degrees.
2. In a large bowl combine egg whites with cream of tartar. Beat until frothy. Slowly add Equal™ while continuing to beat egg whites. Beat until whites are stiff but not dry.
3. Spray a cookie sheet with nonstick spray. Use about 2 heaping tablespoons of egg white mixture per meringue. Place on cookie sheet and hollow out center a bit, creating a shell.
4. Bake for 50 to 60 minutes or until dry and just barely browned. Turn off oven and allow meringues to cool in the oven, if possible, to dry them out even further. If you're not serving them immediately, keep meringues loosely wrapped in a dry place.

Makes 8 meringues. 1 serving = 1 meringue

**Each serving contains:**
- **8 calories**
- **2 grams protein**
- **negligible grams carbohydrate**
- **0 grams fat**
- **25 mgs. sodium**
- **0 mgs. cholesterol**
- **0 grams dietary fiber**

> **ADA Exchange Value**
> **Negligible fat calories.**

# Poached Apples with Almond Meringue

2  *medium apples*
   *Juice of ¹/₂ lemon*
¹/₄  **Meringue recipe (page 150), unbaked**
¹/₂  **teaspoon almond extract**
¹/₄  **cup Chocolate Sauce (page 149)**

1. Preheat oven to 350 degrees.
2. Combine lemon juice with about 1¹/₂ cups water in a saucepan.
3. Core and peel apples. Cut apples in half and place in water and lemon juice. Bring to a boil, reduce heat to a simmer, and cook about 6 minutes or until just tender.
4. Drain apples and cool slightly.
5. Prepare meringue recipe, adding almond extract to egg whites with Equal™.
6. Place apple halves into baking dish, cut side down. Spoon meringue over the top and cover sides to seal. Bake for 20 minutes or until meringue is browned. Cool slightly. Serve, adding 1 tablespoon Chocolate Sauce over top of each serving.

Makes 4 servings.

*Each serving contains:*

36  *calories*
 1  *gram protein*
 7  *grams carbohydrate*
    *negligible grams fat*
25  *mgs. sodium*
 0  *mgs. cholesterol*
 1  *gram dietary fiber*

   *ADA Exchange Value*
¹/₂  *Fruit*
   *Negligible fat calories.*

# Rice Pudding

2 *cups nonfat or 1% milk*
2 *tablespoons fructose*
$^1/_2$ *cup white rice*
$^1/_4$ *cup nonfat evaporated milk, very cold*
$^1/_4$ *cup low-fat sour cream*
1 *teaspoon vanilla*

1. Bring milk to boil in a small pan and be careful not to scorch. Add rice and fructose and stir. Cover, reduce heat, and simmer for about 20 minutes or until rice is done. Remove from heat and cool slightly.
2. Meanwhile, whip nonfat evaporated milk until thick and creamy.
3. In another small bowl combine sour cream and vanilla. Carefully fold into whipped milk.
4. Fold milk and sour cream mixture into rice and gently stir just to mix. Put into serving dishes and garnish with nutmeg or cinnamon.

Makes 6 servings. 1 serving = $^1/_2$ cup

*Each serving contains:*
103 *calories*
4 *grams protein*
17 *grams carbohydrate*
2 *grams fat*
63 *mgs. sodium*
5 *mgs. cholesterol*
0 *grams dietary fiber*

*ADA Exchange Value:*
1 *Starch/Bread*
$^1/_4$ *Fruit*
18% *of total calories are from fat.*

# Apple Muffins

    2  *tablespoons margarine*
   1/4  *cup fructose*
    2  *egg whites*
1 1/2  *cups flour*
   1/4  *teaspoon baking powder*
    1  *cup applesauce, unsweetened*
   1/2  *teaspoon cinnamon*
   1/4  *teaspoon allspice*

1. Cream together margarine and fructose. Stir in egg whites.
2. Sift flour and baking powder together and add to margarine and egg whites. Blend into a dough. Shape dough into a ball, wrap in plastic wrap, and chill at least 1 hour.
3. Preheat oven to 350 degrees. Spray muffin tin with nonstick spray. Cups in muffin tins should measure about 1 inch in diameter.
4. Cut off 1/3 of the dough, rewrap and return to refrigerator. Divide remaining dough into 8 pieces and firmly press each piece onto the bottom and sides of each cup in muffin tin.
5. Combine cinnamon and allspice with applesauce. Fill each muffin with 2 tablespoons of applesauce mixture.
6. Remove rest of dough from the refrigerator and roll out very thin. Cut with a 2 to 2 1/2-inch biscuit cutter and place each round on top of applesauce. Pinch or crimp the top piece to the sides of each muffin in order to seal the edges.
7. Bake 30 to 35 minutes. Muffins should be nicely browned. Allow them to cool in the muffin tins, then remove carefully.

Makes 8 muffins. 1 serving = 1 muffin

*Each serving contains:*

- *139   calories*
- *2   grams protein*
- *25   grams carbohydrate*
- *3   grams fat*
- *66   mgs. sodium*
- *0   mgs. cholesterol*
- *1   gram dietary fiber*

*ADA Exchange Value:*

- *1   Starch/Bread*
- *¹/₂   Fruit*
- *1   Fat*
- *19%   of total calories are from fat.*

# Pound Cake

- 4 tablespoons corn oil margarine
- 1/2 cup fructose
- 4 egg whites
- 1 1/2 cups flour
- 1 teaspoon baking soda
- 3/4 teaspoon cinnamon
- 1 teaspoon cardamon
- 1/2 cup reduced-calorie sour cream
- 1 teaspoon vanilla

1. Preheat oven to 350 degrees. Cream margarine and fructose. Stir in egg whites and mix well. Do not over mix.
2. Sift together flour, soda, cinnamon, and cardamon. Stir 1/2 of flour mixture into margarine mixture.
3. Stir in sour cream, vanilla, and rest of flour. Mix just enough to combine the ingredients. Pour into a loaf pan.
4. Bake about 50 minutes or until baked through. Be careful not to overbake. Cool thoroughly before slicing.

Makes 18 servings.

*Each serving contains:*
- 75 calories
- 2 grams protein
- 12 grams carbohydrate
- 2 grams fat
- 84 mgs. sodium
- 1 mg. cholesterol
- negligible grams dietary fiber

*ADA Exchange Value:*
- 1 Starch/Bread
- 24% of total calories are from fat.

# Scandinavian Fruit Soup

A classic soup that is tasty and different.

> $^1/_2$ **cup dried pitted prunes (about 10)**
> $^1/_2$ **cup dried apricot halves (about 16)**
> $^1/_4$ **cup raisins**
> $^1/_2$ **lemon, sliced**
>   3 **4-inch cinnamon sticks**
>   1 **tablespoon fructose**
> 1 $^1/_2$ **tablespoons quick-cooking tapioca**
>   1 **small apple, cubed**

1. Combine all ingredients except apple in a saucepan.  Add 3 cups water and bring to a boil.  Reduce heat, cover, and simmer for 20 minutes, stirring occasionally.
2. Add apple.  Cover and simmer about 5 minutes.  Turn off heat, remove cinnamon, and cool.  Serve warm or cold.

Makes 6 servings.  1 serving = $^1/_2$ cup

**Each serving contains:**
> 63 *calories*
>  1 *gram protein*
> 17 *grams carbohydrate*
>    *negligible grams fat*
>  2 *mgs. sodium*
>  0 *mgs. cholesterol*
>  2 *grams dietary fiber*

**ADA Exchange Value:**
> 1 *Fruit*
>   *negligible fat calories.*

# Rum Fruitcake

Plan in advance to make this cake.  It needs a week to marinate.
Make several for great holiday gifts.

$^1/_2$  **cup rum**
  1  **6-ounce can frozen orange juice concentrate,
     thawed**
  1  **cup cranberries, chopped**
  1  **8-ounce package dates, pitted and chopped**
$^1/_2$  **cup walnuts, chopped**
  1  **tablespoon orange rind, grated**
  1  **tablespoon vanilla**
  4  **egg whites**
  1  **8-ounce can pineapple tidbits, unsweetened,
     drained**
2 $^1/_4$  **cups flour**
1 $^1/_4$  **teaspoons baking soda**
$^1/_2$  **teaspoon cinnamon**
$^1/_2$  **teaspoon nutmeg**
$^1/_4$  **teaspoon allspice**
$^1/_2$  **cup rum**
$^1/_2$  **cup fresh orange juice**

1. Preheat oven to 325 degrees.
2. Combine $^1/_2$ cup rum, orange juice concentrate, and
   cranberries in a bowl and set aside for 1 hour.
3. Combine the dates, walnuts, orange rind, vanilla, egg whites,
   and pineapple.  Add to the cranberry mixture and stir to mix.
4. In another bowl combine the dry ingredients.  Add to the fruit
   mixture and stir well.
5. Spray a bundt pan with nonstick spray and spoon in batter.
   Bake for 45 minutes or until done in the center.  Let cool about
   20 minutes, then remove from pan.
6. Combine $^1/_2$ cup rum and fresh orange juice.
7. Place cake on a platter or plate.  Place several layers of
   cheesecloth over top of cake.  Pour rum and orange juice
   mixture over cheesecloth.  Wrap the cake and cheesecloth in
   waxed paper or plastic wrap, then in foil.

8. Place cake in a dry place and let sit for one week. Unwrap, slice, and serve.

Makes 24 servings.

*Each serving contains:*
- *101 calories*
- *3 grams protein*
- *14 grams carbohydrate*
- *2 grams fat*
- *67 mgs. sodium*
- *0 mgs. cholesterol*
- *1 gram dietary fiber*

*ADA Exchange Value:*
- *1 Starch/Bread*
- *18% of total calories are from fat.*

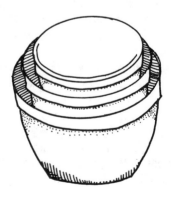

# Raspberry Meringues with Chocolate Sauce

A light, pretty dessert that is very low in calories.

> 1 **cup fresh raspberries, washed and drained**
> 1/2 **Meringue recipe (page 150)**
> 4 **tablespoons Chocolate Sauce (page 149)**

1. Prepare meringue shells according to recipe directions.
2. Carefully place meringue shells onto serving dish. Spoon fresh raspberries into shells and top each with 1 tablespoon of Chocolate Sauce.
3. Garnish with mint, if desired, and serve.

Makes 4 servings.

*Each serving contains:*
> 27 *calories*
> 1 *gram protein*
> 6 *grams carbohydrate*
> 0 *grams fat*
> 30 *mgs. sodium*
> 0 *mgs. cholesterol*
> 2 *grams dietary fiber*

*ADA Exchange Value:*
> 1/2 *Fruit*
> *Negligible fat calories.*

# Russian
# Cuisine

# Russia

Russian cuisine is similar to German and Scandinavian. Russia has a very cold climate so the natives often use root vegetables because they store well or can be pickled. Sour cream is fundamental in Russian cooking. Russians love to entertain in their home and will prepare dishes in advance so they can enjoy the company of their guests. Even though the Russian diet is rather heavy, it is easy to lighten those fat calories with the help of low-fat sour cream. We make a delicious sauce for our Russian dishes by adding low-fat sour cream to our Basic White Sauce.

In Russia no party is complete without vodka. Most Russians will drink it straight, but we mix it with some soda or with a squeeze of lime. Caviar is also a favorite, if your pocketbook and your sodium intake can handle it. There are some palatable caviars on the market that are within a reasonable budget. A little caviar can go a long way, so give it a try at least once!

# A Russian Winter Party

Some parts of Russia have severe winters, so it seems appropriate to plan a taste of Russia party in winter. Make it casual with a showing of *Silk Stockings* on your video.

### Appetizer

Blini with caviar
Vodka and soda

### Soup

Hot Borscht in mugs
Russian rye bread (bought at your bakery)

### Main Course

Beef Stroganoff with Kasha
Vegetable Salad
Braised Carrots

### Dessert

Cheese Curd Pudding
Tea

# Blini (Buckwheat Pancakes)

Blini are served at the end of winter as a sign of sun and spring. They are accompanied by sour cream, caviar, and Russian vodka.

|       |                                |
|------:|--------------------------------|
| 2     | *cups nonfat milk, warmed*     |
| 1     | *tablespoon yeast*             |
| 1 ¹/₃ | *cups flour*                   |
| 1/2   | *cup buckwheat flour*          |
| 1     | *teaspoon fructose*            |
| 4     | *egg whites*                   |
| 2     | *tablespoons melted margarine* |
| ¹/₄   | *cup yogurt cheese*            |
| ¹/₄   | *cup low-fat sour cream*       |
| ¹/₄   | *cup black caviar*             |

1. In 1 cup milk dissolve yeast and add 1 teaspoon flour. Place mixture in a warm place until it rises to double its size.
2. Add the rest of the warmed milk. Sift in the remaining flour, add fructose, 2 egg whites, and margarine. Beat until smooth. Set dough aside to rise until double in size, knead it lightly, and let it rise again.
3. Whisk the remaining egg white until frothy and add to the mixture.
4. Heat a nonstick skillet sprayed with nonstick spray and make 12 pancakes (these will be thicker than normal pancakes).
5. Mix yogurt cheese and sour cream together and place 2 teaspoons on each pancake. Top with 1 teaspoon caviar.

Makes 12 servings.

*Each serving contains:*

- *112 calories*
- *7 grams protein*
- *17 grams carbohydrate*
- *2 grams fat*
- *162 mgs. sodium*
- *9 mgs. cholesterol*
- *1 gram dietary fiber*

*ADA Exchange Value:*

- *1 Starch/Bread*
- *1 Lean Meat*
- *16% of total calories are from fat.*

# Potato Cakes with Mushroom Sauce

1   pound russet potatoes, cubed with skin
2   tablespoons Butter Buds™, dry
2   egg whites
1/2 cup flour

*Sauce:*

6   ounces mushrooms, sliced
1   onion, chopped
1 1/2 cups vegetable stock
1   tablespoon flour

1. Cook potatoes, drain.  Add Butter Buds™ and mash.
2. Mix in egg whites and form into 6 balls.  Flatten balls in flour to coat.
3. In a skillet sprayed with nonstick spray, fry the potato cakes. Top with sauce.

Sauce:

4. Saute mushrooms and onion in a saucepan sprayed with nonstick spray.  Set aside.
5. Mix the vegetable stock and flour together in the skillet and heat, stirring constantly, until thickened.  Add the mushroom and onion to sauce and heat through.

Makes 6 servings.

*Each serving contains:*

119 calories
4   grams protein
25  grams carbohydrate
    negligible grams fat
396 mgs. sodium
    negligible mgs. cholesterol
1   gram dietary fiber

*ADA Exchange Value:*

1   Starch/Bread
1   Vegetable
    negligible fat calories.

EUROPEAN CUISINE FROM THE GUILTLESS GOURMET

# Borscht

5   large beets, peeled and grated
1   medium onion, chopped
6   cups low-salt Chicken Broth (page 53)
1   cup tomato puree
1   tablespoon lemon juice
$^1/_2$   teaspoon freshly ground black pepper
1   teaspoon fructose
1   cup low-fat sour cream

1. Combine beets, onion, and Chicken Broth in a Dutch oven. Bring to boil, reduce heat, cover, and simmer for 45 minutes.
2. Add tomato puree, lemon juice, pepper, and fructose. Simmer another 45 minutes.
3. Pour soup in blender and puree until smooth. Serve hot or cold, topped with sour cream.

Makes 6 servings.

*Each serving contains:*
126   *calories*
5   *grams protein*
17   *grams carbohydrate*
5   *grams fat*
400   *mgs. sodium*
9   *mgs. cholesterol*
4   *grams dietary fiber*

*ADA Exchange Value:*
2   *Vegetable*
1   *Fat*
36%   *of total calories are from fat.*

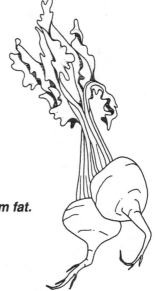

# Russian Red Cabbage

1   medium red cabbage, shredded
1   medium onion, chopped
2   tablespoons vinegar
1   tablespoon molasses
2   green apples, cored and grated
$1/2$   teaspoon ground black pepper
1   cup water

1. Saute onion in a Dutch oven sprayed with nonstick spray.
2. Add remaining ingredients and bring to boil.  Reduce heat,
   cover, and simmer for 1 $1/2$ hours.

Makes 6 servings.

*Each serving contains:*
52   *calories*
1   *gram protein*
13   *grams carbohydrate*
     *negligible grams fat*
11   *mgs. sodium*
0   *mgs. cholesterol*
3   *grams dietary fiber*

*ADA Exchange Value:*
1   *Vegetable*
$1/2$   *Fruit*
     *Negligible fat calories.*

# Braised Carrots

    2   tablespoons Butter Buds™, dry
  ¹/₂   cup water
  ¹/₂   teaspoon fructose
    1   pound carrots, sliced diagonally or cut into
        1 ¹/₂-inch strips

1. In a saucepan mix Butter Buds™, water, and fructose
   together.  Bring to a boil.
2. Add carrots.  Reduce heat to simmer, cover, and cook for 5
   minutes.  Uncover and bring back to a boil and cook until all
   liquid is absorbed.

Makes 6 servings.

**Each serving contains:**
    36   calories
         negligible grams protein
     9   grams carbohydrate
         negligible grams fat
    49   mgs. sodium
     0   mgs. cholesterol
     3   grams dietary fiber

**ADA Exchange Value:**
  1 ¹/₂   Vegetable
         Negligible fat calories.

# Russian Cutlets

12 ounces lean ground beef
12 ounces ground chicken breast
1 ½ cups bread crumbs
1 medium onion, minced
2 tablespoons fresh parsley, chopped
2 egg whites
¼ teaspoon ground black pepper
1 recipe White Sauce (page 104)
¼ cup low-fat sour cream
Chopped fresh parsley for garnish

1. Preheat oven to 350 degrees.
2. Mix ground beef, ground chicken, ½ cup bread crumbs, onion, 2 tablespoons parsley, egg whites, and pepper together.
3. Form 6 balls and roll them in 1 cup bread crumbs. Form the balls into ovals. Place on a cookie sheet that has been sprayed with nonstick spray.
4. Make the White Sauce and add sour cream to it.
5. Serve cutlets with sour cream sauce spooned over them. Sprinkle with chopped parsley.

Makes 6 servings.

*Each serving contains:*
221 calories
20 grams protein
25 grams carbohydrate
4 grams fat
286 mgs. sodium
23 mgs. cholesterol
1 gram dietary fiber

*ADA Exchange Value:*
2 Lean Meat
1 ½ Starch/Bread
16% of total calories are from fat.

# Pancake Pie

*Pancakes:*

|       |                              |
|-------|------------------------------|
| 4     | egg whites                   |
| 1     | teaspoon fructose            |
| 1 1/2 | cups nonfat milk             |
| 1     | cup flour                    |
| 1     | tablespoon melted margarine  |

*Filling:*

|      |                                 |
|------|---------------------------------|
| 12   | ounces lean ground beef         |
| 1    | medium onion, chopped           |
| 6    | ounces mushrooms, sliced        |
| 1    | recipe White Sauce (page 104)   |
| 1/2  | cup low-fat sour cream          |

1. Mix all pancake batter ingredients together in a bowl and set aside.
2. Preheat oven to 300 degrees.
3. Cook meat in a nonstick skillet. Remove meat to a paper plate lined with paper towels to drain off excess fat.
4. Saute onion in the skillet sprayed with nonstick spray. Remove onion to the plate with ground beef.
5. Saute mushrooms in the skillet.
6. Add meat and onion to skillet with the mushrooms. Stir in the White Sauce and sour cream.
7. Make 6 8-inch pancakes. In an 8-inch round deep dish pan sprayed with nonstick spray, layer the pancakes and meat mixture, starting and ending with a pancake.
8. Bake 15 minutes. Turn upside down on a round plate.

Makes 4 servings.

*Each serving contains:*
- *361   calories*
- *32   grams protein*
- *38   grams carbohydrate*
- *8   grams fat*
- *231   mgs. sodium*
- *50   mgs. cholesterol*
- *1   gram dietary fiber*

**ADA Exchange Value:**
- *4   Lean Meat*
- *2   Starch/Bread*
- *20%   of total calories are from fat.*

# Chicken Cutlet Pojarski

12  ounces ground chicken breast
$1/4$  teaspoon grated nutmeg
$1/2$  teaspoon ground white pepper
 4  egg whites
 2  tablespoons water with 1 teaspoon olive oil
$1/2$  cup flour
1 $1/2$  cups bread crumbs

*Sauce:*

 1  recipe White Sauce (page 104)
 2  teaspoons paprika
$1/4$  cup low-fat sour cream
 1  teaspoon cognac

1. Mix ground chicken, nutmeg, pepper, and 2 egg whites together and chill for one-half hour.
2. Preheat oven to 375 degrees.
3. Mix remaining egg whites together with water and olive oil in a pie plate.  Place the flour on a paper plate and the bread crumbs on another.
4. Make 6 balls from the chilled chicken mixture.  Roll each ball first in flour, then egg mixture, and then bread crumbs.
5. Flatten balls out to ovals.  Place them on a cookie sheet sprayed with nonstick spray and bake for 30 minutes or until done.

Sauce:
6. Make White Sauce and mix in the paprika, sour cream, and cognac.
7. Spoon sauce over each cutlet and serve.

Makes 6 servings.

*Each serving contains:*
- 272 *calories*
- 25 *grams protein*
- 32 *grams carbohydrate*
- 3 *grams fat*
- 314 *mgs. sodium*
- 25 *mgs. cholesterol*
- 1 *gram dietary fiber*

*ADA Exchange Value:*
- 2 *Lean Meat*
- 2 *Starch/Bread*
- 10% *of total calories are from fat.*

# Beef Stroganoff

To give this dish a real Russian flair, serve it with Kasha (bulgur wheat).

> 1 *pound lean sirloin steak, cut in strips*
> 1/2 *medium onion, cut in thin strips*
> 1 *pound mushrooms, sliced*
> 1/2 *teaspoon ground white pepper*
> 2 *cups White Sauce (page 104)*
> 1/2 *cup low-fat sour cream*

1. Heat a large nonstick skillet. When hot, add beef and brown it quickly. Remove beef from pan and set aside.
2. Place onions and mushrooms in skillet. Cover, reduce heat to low, and simmer 5 minutes. Remove lid, increase heat, and cook until all liquid is absorbed. Remove onion and mushrooms and set aside.
3. Make the White Sauce in the skillet and add pepper.* Add sour cream.
4. Gently stir in the meat and vegetables and heat through.

*Recipe may be prepared 2 hours ahead to this point.
Makes 6 servings.

*Each serving contains:*
> 182 *calories*
> 22 *grams protein*
> 12 *grams carbohydrate*
> 5 *grams fat*
> 152 *mgs. sodium*
> 26 *mgs. cholesterol*
> 1 *gram dietary fiber*

*ADA Exchange Value:*
> 3 *Lean Meat*
> 2 *Vegetable*
> 25% *of total calories are from fat.*

# Cheese Curd Pudding

1   *pound cheese curd (use dry curd cottage cheese)*
2   *egg whites*
2   *tablespoons fructose*
2   *tablespoons semolina flour*
1   *teaspoon vanilla*
6   *teaspoons sugar-free jam*

1. Preheat oven to 350 degrees.
2. Place all ingredients except jam in a food processor with a steel blade.  Process until smooth.
3. Divide mixture into 6 custard cups that have been sprayed with nonstick spray.
4. Top each cup with 1 teaspoon of jam.  Bake for 15 minutes. Serve cold.

Makes 6 servings.

*Each serving contains:*
87   *calories*
10   *grams protein*
11   *grams carbohydrate*
       *negligible grams fat*
29   *mgs. sodium*
3   *mgs. cholesterol*
       *negligible grams dietary fiber*

*ADA Exchange Value:*
1   *Lean Meat*
1/2   *Fruit*
       *negligible fat calories.*

# Index

Noodle bake, 76

Octoberfest menu, 59
Onion Potato Cake, 110
Orange Tea Loaf, 120
Orzo Pilaf, 34
Oven-Fried Eggplant, 36

Pancake Pie, 171
Pancakes
    buckwheat (Blini), 164
    potato, 72
    Swedish, 131
Pastitsio, 43
Peach Pudding, 51
Pear and Lettuce Salad, 31
Pears in White Sauce, 109
Peppers, stuffed, 45
Pickled Beet Salad, 136
Pickled Fish, 139
Poached Apples with Almond
Meringue, 151
Poached Salmon with Mustard
Dill Sauce, 147
Pork Chops with Potatoes, 83
Pork tenderloin, 84
Potato and onion cake, 110
Potato Cakes with Mushroom
Sauce, 166
Potato dumplings, 73
Potato Leek Soup, 133
Potato Pancakes, 72
Potato salad
    German, 63
    sour cream, 141
Potatoes
    baked stuffed, 111
    roasted, 112
    scalloped, 71
Pound Cake, 155

Pudding
    cheese curd, 176
    peach, 51
    Greek rice, 52
    rice, 152

Quick Scones, 121

Raspberry Meringues with
    Chocolate Sauce, 159
Red cabbage, Russian, 168
Red Cabbage with Apples, 66
Ribs, 85
Rice, 11
Rice Casserole, 144
Rice Pudding, 52, 152
Rice with Onions, 113
Roasted Potatoes, 112
Rum Fruitcake, 157
Russian Cutlets, 170
Russian Red Cabbage, 168
Russian winter party menu,
    163

Salads
    beetroot, 106
    cucumber yogurt, 33
    crab, 107
    fish, 142
    Greek, 30
    green bean, 135
    leek, 64
    mixed vegetable, 105
    mushroom, 143
    pear and lettuce, 31
    pickled beet, 136
    tomato cucumber, 32
Salmon, poached, 147
Salmon Dill Pie, 114
Sandwiches, 96-101

Sauces
  chocolate, 149
  white, 104
Sauerbraten, 89
Scalloped Turnips and
  Potatoes, 71
Scandinavian Cabbage, 138
Scandinavian Fruit Soup, 156
Scones, 121-124
Sherry Trifle, 125
Shish Kebab, 47
Shrimp with Tomato and
  Feta Cheese, 38
Smorgasbord menu, 130
Soups
  asparagus and
    spinach, 102
  cabbage with
    meatballs, 62
  carrot, leek, and
    potato, 103
  chicken and barley, 61
  chicken lemon, 28
  fresh spinach, 134
  potato leek, 133
  Scandinavian fruit, 156
  spinach and lentil, 27
  split pea, 60
  yogurt, 26
Sour cream, 11
Sour Cream Potato Salad, 141
Sour Cream Waffles, 132
Spanakopita, 44
Spatzle, 74
Spinach
  and asparagus soup,
    102
  creamed, 108
Spinach and Lentil Soup, 27
Spinach Cheese Pie
  (Spanakopita), 44
Spinach soup, 134
Split Pea Soup, 60
Sponge Cake, 119
Stuffed Eggplant, 35

Stuffed Peppers, 45
Stuffed Zucchini, 37
Swedish Meatballs, 145
Swedish Pancakes, 131


Tomato Cucumber Salad, 32
Tomato sauce, Greek, 29
Trifle, sherry, 125
Tuna sandwich spread, 98
Turkey Breast Marinated with
  lemon and Herbs, 46
Turnips, scalloped, 71


Veal Schnitzel, 82
Vegetable medleys, 65, 70
Vegetable salad, 105


Waffles, sour cream, 132
Watercress, 97
Whitefish and potatoes, 80
White sauce, 104


Yogurt, 11
Yogurt Cheese, 11, 54
Yogurt Cream, 55
Yogurt Cream, Celery, and
  Walnuts Sandwich
  Spread, 99
Yogurt cucumber salad, 33
Yogurt Soup, 26


Ziti, 43
Zucchini, stuffed, 37

# Recipe Notes

# Recipe Notes

# Recipe Notes

# Recipe Notes

# Recipe Notes

# Recipe Notes

# Recipe Notes

# Recipe Notes

# Recipe Notes

# Recipe Notes

# DCI Publishing Books of Related Interest

**Fast Food Facts** by Marion Franz, RD. This revised and up-to-date best-seller shows how to make smart nutritional choices at fast food restaurants—and tells what to avoid. Includes complete nutrition information on more than 1,000 menu offerings from the 32 largest fast food chains.

| | | | |
|---|---|---|---|
| Standard-size edition | 004068, | ISBN 0-937721-67-0, | $6.95 |
| Pocket edition | 004073, | ISBN 0-937721-69-7, | $4.95 |

**All-American Low-Fat Meals in Minutes** by M.J. Smith, RD, LD, MA. Filled with tantalizing recipes and valuable tips, this cookbook makes great-tasting low-fat foods a snap for holidays, special occasions, or everyday. Most recipes take only minutes to prepare.

004079, ISBN 0-937721-73-5, $12.95

**The Guiltless Gourmet** by Judy Gilliard and Joy Kirkpatrick, RD. A perfect fusion of sound nutrition and creative cooking, this book is loaded with delicious recipes high in flavor and low in fat, sugar, calories, cholesterol, and salt.

004021, ISBN 0937721-23-9, $9.95

**The Guiltless Gourmet Goes Ethnic** by Judy Gilliard and Joy Kirkpatrick, RD. More than a cookbook, this sequel to The Guiltless Gourmet shows how easy it is to lower the sugar, calories, sodium, and fat in your favorite ethnic dishes—without sacrificing taste.

004072, ISBN 0-937721-68-9, $11.95

**Convenience Food Facts** by Marion Franz, RD, MS, and Arlene Monk, RD. Includes complete nutrition information, tips, and exchange values on over 1,500 popular name-brand processed foods commonly found in grocery store freezers and shelves. It helps you plan easy-to-prepare, nutritious meals.

004081, ISBN 0-937721-77-8, $9.95

**Exchanges for All Occasions** by Marion Franz, RD, MS. Exchanges and meal planning suggestions for just about any occasion, sample meal plans, special tips for people with diabetes, and more.

004003, ISBN 0-937721-22-0, $8.95

**Fight Fat & Win** by Elaine Moquette-Magee, RD, MPH. This breakthrough book explains how to easily incorporate low-fat dietary guidelines into every modern eating experience, from fast food and common restaurants to quick meals at home, simply by making smarter choices.

004070, ISBN 0-937721-65-4, $9.95

**Joy of Snacks** by Nancy Cooper, RD. Offers over 200 delicious recipes and nutritional information for hearty snacks including sandwiches, appetizers, soups, spreads, cookies, muffins, and treats especially for kids. The book also suggests guidelines for selecting convenience snacks and interpreting information on food labels.

0004086, ISBN 0-937721-82-4, $12.95

**Opening the Door to Good Nutrition** by Marion Franz, RD, MS, et al. This book is for all of us who want to have healthy eating habits but don't know where to start. It not only provides nutrition facts, but also a step-by-step process for improving eating behavior.

004013,  ISBN 0-937721-15-8,  $7.95

**Pass the Pepper Please** by Diane Reader, RD, and Marion Franz, RD, MS. This imaginative book is loaded with fresh and clear suggestions for cutting back on salt to lower blood pressure and maintain good health.

004020,  ISBN 0-937721-17-4,  $3.95

**The Expresslane Diet** by Audrey Fran Blumenfeld, RD. This 21-day weight-management plan meets U.S. recommended daily allowances using brand name convenience and frozen foods and even some fast foods. With this nutritious diet you'll lose weight quickly—up to seven pounds a week.

004055,  ISBN 0-937721-61-1,  $7.95

*Buy them at your local bookstore or use this convenient coupon for ordering.*

**DCI Publishing**
**P.O. Box 47945**
**Minneapolis, MN 55447-9727**

Please send me the books I have checked above. I am enclosing $_____. (Please add $2.50 to this order to cover postage and handling. Minnesota residents add 6% sales tax.) Send check of money order, no cash or C.O.D.'s. Prices are subject to change without notice.

Name _____

Address _____

City _____ State _____ Zip Code_____

Allow 4 to 6 weeks for delivery.
Quantity discounts available upon request.

**Or order by phone: 1-800-848-2793,**
**1-800-444-5951 (non-metro area of Minnesota)**
**612-541-0239 (Minneapolis/St. Paul metro area).**

**Please have your credit card number ready.**